70 Rice and Grain Recipes for Home

By: Kelly Johnson

Table of Contents

Rice Dishes:
- Classic Fried Rice
- Lemon Garlic Butter Rice
- Mushroom Risotto
- Coconut Rice with Pineapple
- Spanish Paella
- Teriyaki Chicken and Vegetable Rice Bowl
- Shrimp and Saffron Rice
- Cajun Dirty Rice
- Greek Lemon Rice Pilaf
- Thai Basil Chicken Fried Rice

Quinoa Creations:
- Quinoa Salad with Avocado and Black Beans
- Mediterranean Quinoa Bowl
- Quinoa Stuffed Bell Peppers
- Lemon Herb Quinoa
- Cranberry Pecan Quinoa Pilaf
- Quinoa and Vegetable Stir-Fry
- Southwest Quinoa Casserole
- Spinach and Feta Quinoa Cakes
- Quinoa Chili
- Teriyaki Salmon with Quinoa

Barley Beauties:
- Mushroom Barley Soup
- Barley Risotto with Asparagus and Parmesan
- Mediterranean Barley Salad
- Beef and Barley Stew
- Barley and Vegetable Stir-Fry
- Barley and Lentil Pilaf
- Barley and Chickpea Bowl
- Lemon Barley Water
- Barley and Roasted Butternut Squash
- Barley and Sausage Skillet

Couscous Concoctions:
- Lemon Herb Couscous

- Mediterranean Couscous Salad
- Couscous-stuffed Peppers
- Shrimp and Vegetable Couscous
- Moroccan Spiced Chicken with Couscous
- Greek-Style Couscous with Tomatoes and Feta
- Couscous with Roasted Vegetables
- Harissa Chickpea Couscous
- Couscous Tabbouleh
- Spicy Sausage and Spinach Couscous

Wild Rice Wonders:

- Wild Rice Pilaf with Cranberries and Almonds
- Chicken and Wild Rice Soup
- Mushroom and Spinach Stuffed Acorn Squash with Wild Rice
- Wild Rice and Turkey Meatballs
- Wild Rice and Roasted Vegetable Salad
- Creamy Wild Mushroom RIsotto with Truffle Oil
- Wild Rice and Quinoa Cakes
- Orange Pecan Wild Rice
- Lemon Garlic Shrimp with Wild Rice
- Turkey and Cranberry Stuffed Bell Peppers with Wild Rice

Millet Marvels:

- Millet and BLack Bean Salad
- Millet-Stuffed Portobello Mushrooms
- Lemon Millet Pilaf
- Millet and Vegetable Stir-Fry
- Millet Patties with Avocado Sauce
- Creamy Pumpkin Millet Porridge
- Millet and Kale Soup
- Millet and Roasted Butternut Squash Bowl
- Millet Tabbouleh
- Millet and Chickpea Buddha Bowl

Farro Feasts:

- Farro and Vegetable Stir-Fry
- Farro and Italian Sausage Stuffed Peppers
- Lemon Garlic Shrimp with Farro
- Farro Salad with Roasted Vegetables and Feta
- Creamy Mushroom and Spinach Farro Risotto
- Farro and Pomegranate Salad
- Farro and Lentil Soup

- Mediterranean Farro Bowl
- Chicken and Farro Skillet
- Farro and Asparagus Risotto

Rice Dishes:
Classic Fried Rice

Ingredients:

- 2 cups cooked jasmine or long-grain white rice (preferably a day old and chilled)
- 2 tablespoons vegetable oil
- 2 eggs, lightly beaten
- 1 cup mixed vegetables (peas, carrots, corn, and/or diced bell peppers)
- 1/2 cup diced cooked chicken, shrimp, or tofu (optional)
- 3 green onions, finely chopped
- 3 tablespoons soy sauce
- 1 tablespoon oyster sauce
- 1 teaspoon sesame oil
- 1/2 teaspoon sugar
- Salt and pepper to taste

Instructions:

Prepare Ingredients:
- Make sure all your ingredients are chopped and ready before you start cooking.
- If using day-old rice, break up any clumps with your hands.

Cook the Eggs:
- Heat a large skillet or wok over medium-high heat.
- Add 1 tablespoon of vegetable oil to the pan.
- Pour the beaten eggs into the pan and scramble them until just set.
- Remove the eggs from the pan and set aside.

Stir-Fry Vegetables:
- In the same pan, add the remaining tablespoon of vegetable oil.
- Add the mixed vegetables to the pan and stir-fry for 2-3 minutes until they are slightly tender.

Add Protein (Optional):
- If using chicken, shrimp, or tofu, add it to the pan with the vegetables and cook until it's heated through.

Combine with Rice:
- Add the chilled, cooked rice to the pan, breaking up any clumps.
- Stir-fry the rice with the vegetables and protein for 2-3 minutes.

Seasoning:

- In a small bowl, mix together soy sauce, oyster sauce, sesame oil, and sugar.
- Pour the sauce over the rice mixture and stir to combine.

Finish and Serve:
- Add the scrambled eggs back to the pan and stir to combine.
- Season with salt and pepper to taste.
- Stir in chopped green onions.
- Cook for an additional 1-2 minutes until everything is heated through.
- Serve hot and enjoy your classic fried rice!

Feel free to customize this recipe by adding other ingredients like diced ham, bean sprouts, or different sauces to suit your taste preferences.

Lemon Garlic Butter Rice

Ingredients:

- 1 cup long-grain white rice
- 2 cups chicken or vegetable broth
- 2 tablespoons unsalted butter
- 3 cloves garlic, minced
- Zest of 1 lemon
- Juice of 1 lemon
- Salt and pepper to taste
- Fresh parsley, chopped (for garnish)

Instructions:

Rinse the Rice:
- Rinse the rice under cold water until the water runs clear. This helps remove excess starch and prevents the rice from becoming too sticky.

Cook the Rice:
- In a medium saucepan, combine the rinsed rice and chicken or vegetable broth.
- Bring the mixture to a boil, then reduce the heat to low, cover, and simmer for about 15-20 minutes or until the rice is cooked and the liquid is absorbed.

Prepare the Lemon Garlic Butter Sauce:
- While the rice is cooking, melt the butter in a small saucepan over medium heat.
- Add minced garlic to the melted butter and sauté for 1-2 minutes until the garlic becomes fragrant. Be careful not to let it brown.

Combine Lemon Zest and Juice:
- Add the lemon zest and lemon juice to the garlic butter mixture. Stir well to combine.

Fluff the Rice:
- Once the rice is cooked, remove it from the heat and let it sit, covered, for 5 minutes.
- Fluff the rice with a fork to separate the grains.

Combine Rice and Lemon Garlic Butter Sauce:
- Pour the lemon garlic butter sauce over the cooked rice and gently toss to coat the rice evenly with the flavorful mixture.

Season and Garnish:
- Season the lemon garlic butter rice with salt and pepper to taste.
- Garnish with chopped fresh parsley for added color and flavor.

Serve:
- Serve the Lemon Garlic Butter Rice as a side dish to accompany your favorite protein or enjoy it on its own.

This dish provides a bright and zesty flavor with the combination of lemon and garlic, making it a delightful addition to your meals.

Mushroom Risotto

Ingredients:

- 1 1/2 cups Arborio rice
- 4 cups chicken or vegetable broth, kept warm
- 1 cup dry white wine
- 1 cup mushrooms (cremini or button), sliced
- 1/2 cup dried porcini mushrooms, rehydrated in hot water and chopped (reserve the soaking liquid)
- 1 small onion, finely chopped
- 2 cloves garlic, minced
- 1/2 cup Parmesan cheese, grated
- 2 tablespoons unsalted butter
- 2 tablespoons olive oil
- Salt and pepper to taste
- Fresh parsley, chopped (for garnish)

Instructions:

Prepare Mushrooms:
- In a pan, heat 1 tablespoon of olive oil over medium heat.
- Sauté the sliced mushrooms until they are browned and any released liquid has evaporated. Set aside.

Rehydrate Porcini Mushrooms:
- Place the dried porcini mushrooms in a bowl and cover them with hot water. Let them sit for about 15 minutes to rehydrate. Strain and reserve the soaking liquid. Chop the rehydrated porcini mushrooms.

Start the Risotto Base:
- In a large, wide saucepan, heat 1 tablespoon of olive oil over medium heat.
- Add chopped onions and cook until they become translucent.

Toast the Rice:
- Add Arborio rice to the pan and cook for 2-3 minutes, stirring frequently, until the edges of the rice are translucent.

Deglaze with Wine:
- Pour in the dry white wine and stir until most of the liquid has been absorbed by the rice.

Add Mushrooms:

- Stir in the sautéed mushrooms and chopped rehydrated porcini mushrooms.

Begin Adding Broth:
- Begin adding the warm broth one ladle at a time, stirring continuously. Wait until most of the liquid has been absorbed before adding the next ladle.

Use Porcini Soaking Liquid:
- Add some of the reserved porcini soaking liquid to enhance the mushroom flavor.

Continue Cooking:
- Continue this process of adding broth and stirring until the rice is creamy and cooked to al dente, usually around 18-20 minutes.

Finish the Risotto:
- Stir in grated Parmesan cheese and butter.
- Season with salt and pepper to taste.

Serve:
- Garnish with chopped fresh parsley.
- Serve the mushroom risotto hot, with an extra sprinkle of Parmesan on top if desired.

This Mushroom Risotto is rich, creamy, and full of earthy mushroom flavor. Enjoy it as a comforting main dish or as a side to complement your favorite protein.

Coconut Rice with Pineapple

Ingredients:

- 1 cup jasmine or basmati rice
- 1 cup coconut milk
- 1 cup water
- 1 cup fresh pineapple, diced
- 2 tablespoons unsweetened shredded coconut
- 1 tablespoon coconut oil
- 1/2 teaspoon salt
- 1 tablespoon sugar (optional, for a slightly sweet flavor)
- Fresh cilantro or mint for garnish (optional)

Instructions:

Rinse the Rice:
- Rinse the rice under cold water until the water runs clear. This helps remove excess starch.

Prepare Coconut Mixture:
- In a saucepan, combine the coconut milk, water, coconut oil, salt, and sugar (if using). Bring the mixture to a gentle boil over medium heat.

Add Rice:
- Stir in the rinsed rice and reduce the heat to low.

Simmer:
- Cover the saucepan with a tight-fitting lid and let the rice simmer on low heat for 15-20 minutes or until the liquid is absorbed and the rice is tender.

Fluff the Rice:
- Once the rice is cooked, fluff it with a fork to separate the grains.

Add Pineapple:
- Gently fold in the diced pineapple and shredded coconut.

Let it Sit:
- Cover the saucepan again and let it sit for a few minutes to allow the flavors to meld and the pineapple to warm through.

Serve:
- Transfer the coconut rice with pineapple to a serving dish.
- Garnish with fresh cilantro or mint if desired.

This Coconut Rice with Pineapple is a tropical and flavorful side dish that pairs well with a variety of main courses, especially grilled or roasted meats and seafood. Enjoy the sweet and savory combination!

Spanish Paella

Ingredients:

- 2 cups Bomba or Calasparra rice (short-grain rice)
- 4 cups chicken broth
- 1 pound chicken thighs, bone-in and skin-on
- 1/2 pound rabbit, cut into pieces (optional)
- 1/2 pound large shrimp, peeled and deveined
- 1/2 pound mussels, cleaned and debearded
- 1/2 cup extra virgin olive oil
- 1 onion, finely chopped
- 4 cloves garlic, minced
- 1 tomato, grated
- 1/2 cup green beans, trimmed and cut into 2-inch pieces
- 1/2 cup lima beans or peas
- 1 teaspoon smoked paprika (pimentón)
- 1/2 teaspoon saffron threads, soaked in 2 tablespoons warm water
- Salt and pepper to taste
- Lemon wedges for serving

Instructions:

Prepare Ingredients:
- Season the chicken thighs with salt and pepper.
- Soak the saffron threads in warm water.

Preheat:
- Preheat a paella pan or a wide, shallow skillet over medium heat.

Brown the Meat:
- Add olive oil to the pan. Brown the chicken thighs on both sides. If using rabbit, brown it as well. Remove the browned meat and set it aside.

Sauté Aromatics:
- In the same pan, add chopped onions and cook until they are translucent. Add minced garlic and cook for an additional 1-2 minutes.

Add Grated Tomato:
- Stir in the grated tomato and cook until it's softened and the liquid has evaporated.

Add Vegetables:
- Add green beans and lima beans (or peas) to the pan. Stir to combine.

Add Rice and Paprika:
- Sprinkle the rice evenly over the pan. Add smoked paprika and stir everything together.

Pour Broth:
- Pour in the chicken broth and saffron-infused water. Bring to a gentle boil.

Arrange the Meat and Seafood:
- Arrange the browned chicken and rabbit pieces on top of the rice. Nestle the shrimp and mussels into the rice.

Simmer:
- Reduce the heat to low and simmer for about 20-25 minutes, or until the rice is cooked and has formed a crust on the bottom known as "socarrat."

Check for Doneness:
- Make sure the shrimp are cooked, the mussels have opened, and the rice is tender.

Rest and Serve:
- Remove the paella from the heat, cover it with a clean kitchen towel, and let it rest for 5 minutes.
- Serve the Spanish Paella hot, garnished with lemon wedges.

Enjoy the rich and flavorful Spanish Paella as a festive main course!

Teriyaki Chicken and Vegetable Rice Bowl

Ingredients:

For Teriyaki Chicken:

- 1 pound boneless, skinless chicken thighs, cut into bite-sized pieces
- 1/2 cup soy sauce
- 1/4 cup mirin (sweet rice wine)
- 2 tablespoons honey
- 1 tablespoon rice vinegar
- 1 teaspoon sesame oil
- 2 cloves garlic, minced
- 1 teaspoon fresh ginger, grated
- 1 tablespoon cornstarch (optional, for thickening)

For Vegetables:

- 2 cups broccoli florets
- 1 red bell pepper, thinly sliced
- 1 carrot, julienned
- 1 tablespoon vegetable oil

For Rice:

- 2 cups cooked jasmine or short-grain white rice

Garnish:

- Sesame seeds
- Sliced green onions

Instructions:

   Prepare Teriyaki Sauce:
   - In a bowl, whisk together soy sauce, mirin, honey, rice vinegar, sesame oil, minced garlic, and grated ginger. If you prefer a thicker sauce, mix in cornstarch as well.

   Marinate Chicken:

- Place the chicken pieces in a bowl and pour half of the teriyaki sauce over them. Allow it to marinate for at least 15-30 minutes.

Cook Chicken:
- Heat a large skillet or wok over medium-high heat. Add a bit of oil if needed.
- Add the marinated chicken and cook until browned and cooked through. If desired, pour in the remaining teriyaki sauce during the last few minutes of cooking. This will create a glaze on the chicken.

Cook Vegetables:
- In another pan, stir-fry the broccoli, red bell pepper, and julienned carrot in vegetable oil until they are tender-crisp.

Assemble Rice Bowl:
- Divide the cooked rice among serving bowls.
- Top the rice with the cooked teriyaki chicken and stir-fried vegetables.

Garnish and Serve:
- Garnish with sesame seeds and sliced green onions.
- Drizzle with any remaining teriyaki sauce for extra flavor.

Serve Hot:
- Serve the Teriyaki Chicken and Vegetable Rice Bowl immediately while it's hot.

Enjoy this flavorful and satisfying Teriyaki Chicken and Vegetable Rice Bowl!

Shrimp and Saffron Rice

Ingredients:

- 1 cup long-grain white rice
- 2 cups chicken broth
- 1/2 teaspoon saffron threads
- 2 tablespoons warm water
- 1 pound large shrimp, peeled and deveined
- 2 tablespoons olive oil
- 1 onion, finely chopped
- 2 cloves garlic, minced
- 1 red bell pepper, diced
- 1 tomato, diced
- 1/2 teaspoon smoked paprika
- 1/2 teaspoon cayenne pepper (adjust to taste)
- Salt and black pepper to taste
- Fresh parsley, chopped (for garnish)

Instructions:

Prepare Saffron:
- In a small bowl, steep saffron threads in warm water and set aside.

Cook the Rice:
- Rinse the rice under cold water until the water runs clear.
- In a saucepan, bring the chicken broth to a boil. Add the rinsed rice, reduce heat to low, cover, and simmer for about 15-20 minutes or until the rice is cooked and the liquid is absorbed.

Marinate Shrimp:
- In a bowl, combine the peeled and deveined shrimp with a bit of olive oil, salt, and black pepper. Set aside.

Sauté Vegetables:
- In a large skillet, heat the remaining olive oil over medium heat. Add chopped onions and cook until softened.
- Add minced garlic and diced red bell pepper. Sauté for another 2-3 minutes until the vegetables are tender.

Add Tomatoes and Spices:
- Stir in diced tomatoes, smoked paprika, and cayenne pepper. Cook for an additional 2-3 minutes.

Cook Shrimp:
- Push the vegetables to the side of the skillet and add the marinated shrimp. Cook for 2-3 minutes on each side until they turn pink and opaque.

Combine with Rice:
- Once the shrimp is cooked, add the cooked rice to the skillet. Pour the saffron-infused water over the rice and gently toss everything together to combine.

Adjust Seasoning:
- Season the shrimp and saffron rice with salt and black pepper according to taste.

Garnish and Serve:
- Garnish with chopped fresh parsley.
- Serve the Shrimp and Saffron Rice hot, either in a large serving dish or individual plates.

This dish offers a wonderful combination of flavors from the saffron-infused rice and perfectly cooked shrimp. Enjoy your Shrimp and Saffron Rice!

Cajun Dirty Rice

Ingredients:

- 1 cup long-grain white rice
- 2 cups chicken broth
- 1 pound ground pork or ground beef
- 1 onion, finely chopped
- 1 bell pepper, finely chopped
- 2 celery stalks, finely chopped
- 3 cloves garlic, minced
- 1 cup chicken livers, finely chopped (optional)
- 1 tablespoon Cajun seasoning
- 1/2 teaspoon thyme
- 1/2 teaspoon oregano
- 1/2 teaspoon paprika
- 1/4 teaspoon cayenne pepper (adjust to taste)
- Salt and black pepper to taste
- 3 green onions, sliced (for garnish)
- Fresh parsley, chopped (for garnish)

Instructions:

Cook the Rice:
- Rinse the rice under cold water until the water runs clear.
- In a saucepan, bring the chicken broth to a boil. Add the rinsed rice, reduce heat to low, cover, and simmer for about 15-20 minutes or until the rice is cooked and the liquid is absorbed.

Brown the Meat:
- In a large skillet or Dutch oven, brown the ground pork or beef over medium heat. Drain excess fat if needed.

Sauté Vegetables:
- Add chopped onions, bell peppers, celery, and minced garlic to the skillet. Sauté until the vegetables are softened.

Add Chicken Livers (Optional):
- If using chicken livers, add them to the skillet and cook until they are no longer pink in the center.

Seasoning:

- Stir in Cajun seasoning, thyme, oregano, paprika, cayenne pepper, salt, and black pepper. Mix well to coat the meat and vegetables with the spices.

Combine with Rice:
- Add the cooked rice to the skillet and mix everything together. Ensure the rice is well-coated with the flavorful mixture.

Adjust Seasoning:
- Taste and adjust the seasoning if needed. Cajun dishes often have bold flavors, so feel free to add more Cajun seasoning or cayenne pepper to your liking.

Garnish and Serve:
- Garnish the Cajun Dirty Rice with sliced green onions and chopped fresh parsley.
- Serve hot, either as a side dish or a main course.

Enjoy this hearty and spicy Cajun Dirty Rice, a classic Southern dish that's bursting with flavor!

Greek Lemon Rice Pilaf

Ingredients:

- 1 cup long-grain white rice
- 2 cups chicken or vegetable broth
- Zest of 1 lemon
- Juice of 2 lemons
- 2 tablespoons olive oil
- 1 small onion, finely chopped
- 2 cloves garlic, minced
- 1/2 teaspoon dried oregano
- 1 bay leaf
- Salt and black pepper to taste
- Fresh parsley, chopped (for garnish)

Instructions:

Rinse the Rice:
- Rinse the rice under cold water until the water runs clear. This helps remove excess starch.

Prepare Lemon Mixture:
- In a bowl, combine the lemon zest and lemon juice. Set aside.

Sauté Onion and Garlic:
- In a saucepan, heat olive oil over medium heat. Add chopped onions and cook until they become translucent.
- Add minced garlic and sauté for an additional 1-2 minutes until fragrant.

Add Rice and Spices:
- Stir in the rinsed rice, dried oregano, and bay leaf. Cook for 2-3 minutes, stirring occasionally, until the rice is lightly toasted.

Pour Lemon Mixture:
- Pour the lemon zest and juice mixture over the rice. Stir to combine.

Add Broth:
- Pour in the chicken or vegetable broth. Season with salt and black pepper to taste.

Simmer:
- Bring the mixture to a boil, then reduce the heat to low, cover the saucepan, and simmer for about 15-20 minutes or until the rice is cooked, and the liquid is absorbed.

Fluff the Rice:
- Once the rice is cooked, remove the bay leaf and fluff the rice with a fork to separate the grains.

Garnish and Serve:
- Garnish the Greek Lemon Rice Pilaf with chopped fresh parsley.
- Serve hot as a side dish to grilled chicken, fish, or any Mediterranean-inspired main course.

This Greek Lemon Rice Pilaf is light, flavorful, and makes a perfect accompaniment to various Greek and Mediterranean dishes. Enjoy!

Thai Basil Chicken Fried Rice

Ingredients:

- 2 cups cooked jasmine rice (preferably a day old and chilled)
- 1 cup cooked and shredded chicken breast
- 2 tablespoons vegetable oil
- 3 cloves garlic, minced
- 1 red chili, finely chopped (adjust to taste)
- 1 bell pepper, diced
- 1 cup broccoli florets, blanched
- 1 carrot, julienned
- 1/2 cup frozen peas, thawed
- 2 tablespoons soy sauce
- 1 tablespoon oyster sauce
- 1 teaspoon fish sauce
- 1 teaspoon sugar
- 1 cup Thai basil leaves, loosely packed
- Lime wedges for serving
- Fried eggs (optional, for serving)

Instructions:

Prepare Ingredients:
- Ensure all ingredients are chopped and ready before you start cooking.

Heat the Wok or Skillet:
- Heat vegetable oil in a wok or large skillet over medium-high heat.

Sauté Aromatics:
- Add minced garlic and chopped red chili to the hot oil. Stir-fry for about 30 seconds until fragrant.

Add Chicken:
- Add the shredded chicken to the wok and stir-fry until it's heated through.

Add Vegetables:
- Add diced bell pepper, julienned carrot, blanched broccoli, and thawed peas to the wok. Stir-fry for 2-3 minutes until the vegetables are slightly tender.

Stir in Rice:
- Add the chilled, cooked jasmine rice to the wok. Break up any clumps and stir-fry to combine with the chicken and vegetables.

Combine Sauces:
- In a small bowl, mix together soy sauce, oyster sauce, fish sauce, and sugar. Pour the sauce over the rice mixture and stir to coat evenly.

Add Thai Basil:
- Add Thai basil leaves to the wok and stir until they are just wilted.

Taste and Adjust:
- Taste the fried rice and adjust the seasoning if needed, adding more soy sauce or fish sauce according to your preference.

Serve:
- Serve the Thai Basil Chicken Fried Rice hot, garnished with lime wedges.
- Optionally, serve with a fried egg on top for an extra layer of flavor.

Enjoy the aromatic and flavorful Thai Basil Chicken Fried Rice as a delicious and satisfying meal!

Quinoa Creations:
Quinoa Salad with Avocado and Black Beans

Ingredients:

- 1 cup quinoa, rinsed
- 2 cups water or vegetable broth
- 1 can (15 oz) black beans, drained and rinsed
- 1 large avocado, diced
- 1 cup cherry tomatoes, halved
- 1/2 cup red onion, finely chopped
- 1/4 cup fresh cilantro, chopped
- 1/4 cup fresh lime juice (about 2 limes)
- 2 tablespoons extra-virgin olive oil
- 1 clove garlic, minced
- 1 teaspoon ground cumin
- Salt and pepper to taste

Instructions:

Cook Quinoa:
- In a medium saucepan, combine the quinoa and water or vegetable broth. Bring to a boil, then reduce heat to low, cover, and simmer for 15-20 minutes, or until the quinoa is cooked and the liquid is absorbed. Fluff the quinoa with a fork and let it cool.

Prepare Dressing:
- In a small bowl, whisk together lime juice, olive oil, minced garlic, ground cumin, salt, and pepper to make the dressing.

Assemble Salad:
- In a large mixing bowl, combine the cooked and cooled quinoa, black beans, diced avocado, cherry tomatoes, red onion, and chopped cilantro.

Add Dressing:
- Pour the dressing over the salad ingredients and gently toss until everything is well coated.

Chill and Serve:
- Refrigerate the quinoa salad for at least 30 minutes before serving to allow the flavors to meld.

Garnish and Enjoy:

- Before serving, garnish the salad with additional cilantro and lime wedges if desired.

This Quinoa Salad with Avocado and Black Beans makes a nutritious and delicious meal on its own or a fantastic side dish for grilled chicken or fish. Enjoy its vibrant colors and fresh flavors!

Mediterranean Quinoa Bowl

Ingredients:

For Quinoa:

- 1 cup quinoa, rinsed
- 2 cups vegetable broth or water
- Salt to taste

For Mediterranean Bowl:

- 1 cup cherry tomatoes, halved
- 1 cucumber, diced
- 1/2 red onion, finely chopped
- 1/2 cup Kalamata olives, sliced
- 1/2 cup feta cheese, crumbled
- 1/4 cup fresh parsley, chopped

For Lemon Herb Dressing:

- 1/4 cup extra-virgin olive oil
- 2 tablespoons fresh lemon juice
- 1 clove garlic, minced
- 1 teaspoon dried oregano
- Salt and pepper to taste

Optional Protein:

- Grilled chicken, shrimp, or chickpeas

Instructions:

Cook Quinoa:
- In a medium saucepan, combine quinoa, vegetable broth or water, and a pinch of salt. Bring to a boil, then reduce heat to low, cover, and simmer for 15-20 minutes or until quinoa is cooked and liquid is absorbed. Fluff with a fork and let it cool.

Prepare Lemon Herb Dressing:

- In a small bowl, whisk together olive oil, lemon juice, minced garlic, dried oregano, salt, and pepper to make the dressing.

Assemble Mediterranean Bowl:
- In a large bowl, combine the cooked quinoa, cherry tomatoes, diced cucumber, chopped red onion, sliced Kalamata olives, crumbled feta cheese, and chopped fresh parsley.

Add Lemon Herb Dressing:
- Pour the lemon herb dressing over the quinoa and vegetable mixture. Toss gently to combine, ensuring everything is well coated with the dressing.

Optional Protein:
- If desired, add grilled chicken, shrimp, or chickpeas on top for added protein.

Chill and Serve:
- Refrigerate the Mediterranean Quinoa Bowl for about 30 minutes before serving to enhance the flavors.

Garnish and Enjoy:
- Before serving, garnish with additional fresh parsley and a wedge of lemon.
- Serve the Mediterranean Quinoa Bowl as a light and nutritious meal.

This Mediterranean Quinoa Bowl is not only delicious but also packed with fresh, vibrant ingredients. It's a perfect option for a healthy and satisfying lunch or dinner.

Quinoa Stuffed Bell Peppers

Ingredients:

- 4 large bell peppers, halved and seeds removed
- 1 cup quinoa, rinsed
- 2 cups vegetable broth or water
- 1 tablespoon olive oil
- 1 onion, finely chopped
- 2 cloves garlic, minced
- 1 zucchini, diced
- 1 carrot, grated
- 1 can (15 oz) black beans, drained and rinsed
- 1 cup corn kernels (fresh, frozen, or canned)
- 1 teaspoon ground cumin
- 1 teaspoon chili powder
- Salt and pepper to taste
- 1 cup tomato sauce
- 1 cup shredded cheese (cheddar, mozzarella, or a blend)
- Fresh cilantro or parsley, chopped (for garnish)

Instructions:

Preheat the Oven:
- Preheat your oven to 375°F (190°C).

Prepare Bell Peppers:
- Cut the bell peppers in half lengthwise and remove the seeds and membranes. Place the pepper halves in a baking dish.

Cook Quinoa:
- In a saucepan, combine quinoa and vegetable broth or water. Bring to a boil, then reduce heat, cover, and simmer for 15-20 minutes, or until quinoa is cooked and liquid is absorbed. Fluff with a fork and set aside.

Sauté Vegetables:
- In a large skillet, heat olive oil over medium heat. Add chopped onion and garlic, sauté until softened.
- Add diced zucchini, grated carrot, black beans, and corn. Cook for 5-7 minutes until the vegetables are tender.

Seasoning:

- Stir in ground cumin, chili powder, salt, and pepper. Adjust seasoning to taste.

Combine Quinoa and Vegetable Mixture:
- Add the cooked quinoa to the skillet with the sautéed vegetables. Mix well to combine.

Stuff the Bell Peppers:
- Spoon the quinoa and vegetable mixture into each bell pepper half, pressing it down gently.

Top with Tomato Sauce and Cheese:
- Pour tomato sauce over the stuffed peppers, and then sprinkle shredded cheese on top.

Bake:
- Cover the baking dish with aluminum foil and bake in the preheated oven for 25-30 minutes, or until the peppers are tender.

Broil (Optional):
- If you like a golden, bubbly cheese crust, uncover the peppers and broil for an additional 2-3 minutes until the cheese is lightly browned.

Garnish and Serve:
- Remove from the oven, garnish with chopped cilantro or parsley, and serve hot.

These Quinoa Stuffed Bell Peppers make a nutritious and satisfying meal. Enjoy the blend of flavors and textures!

Lemon Herb Quinoa

Ingredients:

- 1 cup quinoa, rinsed
- 2 cups vegetable broth or water
- Zest of 1 lemon
- Juice of 1 lemon
- 2 tablespoons extra-virgin olive oil
- 2 cloves garlic, minced
- 1 teaspoon dried thyme
- 1 teaspoon dried rosemary
- Salt and pepper to taste
- Fresh parsley, chopped (for garnish)

Instructions:

Cook Quinoa:
- In a saucepan, combine quinoa and vegetable broth or water. Bring to a boil, then reduce heat to low, cover, and simmer for 15-20 minutes or until quinoa is cooked and liquid is absorbed. Fluff with a fork and let it cool.

Prepare Lemon Herb Dressing:
- In a small bowl, whisk together the olive oil, lemon zest, lemon juice, minced garlic, dried thyme, dried rosemary, salt, and pepper.

Combine Quinoa and Dressing:
- Once the quinoa has cooled slightly, transfer it to a large bowl.
- Pour the lemon herb dressing over the quinoa and toss to coat evenly.

Adjust Seasoning:
- Taste the lemon herb quinoa and adjust the seasoning if needed, adding more salt, pepper, or lemon juice according to your preference.

Garnish and Serve:
- Garnish the lemon herb quinoa with chopped fresh parsley before serving.
- Serve it as a side dish or a base for grilled vegetables, roasted chicken, or your favorite protein.

This Lemon Herb Quinoa is light, refreshing, and versatile. It makes a great accompaniment to a variety of dishes and is perfect for those looking for a bright and herby flavor in their quinoa. Enjoy!

Cranberry Pecan Quinoa Pilaf

Ingredients:

- 1 cup quinoa, rinsed
- 2 cups vegetable broth or water
- 1/2 cup dried cranberries
- 1/2 cup pecans, chopped
- 1 tablespoon olive oil
- 1 small onion, finely chopped
- 2 cloves garlic, minced
- 1/2 teaspoon dried thyme
- Salt and pepper to taste
- Fresh parsley, chopped (for garnish)

Instructions:

Cook Quinoa:
- In a saucepan, combine quinoa and vegetable broth or water. Bring to a boil, then reduce heat to low, cover, and simmer for 15-20 minutes or until quinoa is cooked and liquid is absorbed. Fluff with a fork and let it cool.

Prepare Cranberries and Pecans:
- While the quinoa is cooking, soak the dried cranberries in warm water for about 10 minutes to plump them up. Drain and set aside.
- Toast the chopped pecans in a dry skillet over medium heat until fragrant. Be careful not to burn them. Set aside.

Sauté Onion and Garlic:
- In a large skillet, heat olive oil over medium heat. Add chopped onion and cook until softened.
- Add minced garlic and cook for an additional 1-2 minutes until fragrant.

Combine Ingredients:
- Add the cooked quinoa to the skillet with sautéed onions and garlic. Mix well.

Add Cranberries and Pecans:
- Stir in the plumped dried cranberries and toasted pecans.

Seasoning:
- Season the quinoa pilaf with dried thyme, salt, and pepper. Adjust seasoning to taste.

Garnish and Serve:
- Garnish the Cranberry Pecan Quinoa Pilaf with chopped fresh parsley before serving.
- Serve it as a side dish or enjoy it on its own for a light and flavorful meal.

This Cranberry Pecan Quinoa Pilaf offers a delightful combination of sweet and savory flavors with a hint of nuttiness. It's perfect for holiday meals or any time you want a wholesome and tasty dish. Enjoy!

Quinoa and Vegetable Stir-Fry

Ingredients:

- 1 cup quinoa, rinsed
- 2 cups water or vegetable broth
- 2 tablespoons soy sauce
- 1 tablespoon hoisin sauce
- 1 tablespoon rice vinegar
- 1 tablespoon sesame oil
- 1 tablespoon vegetable oil
- 2 cloves garlic, minced
- 1 tablespoon ginger, grated
- 1 bell pepper, thinly sliced
- 1 carrot, julienned
- 1 zucchini, sliced
- 1 cup broccoli florets
- 1 cup snap peas, trimmed
- 1 cup tofu or cooked chicken, diced (optional)
- Green onions, chopped, for garnish
- Sesame seeds, for garnish

Instructions:

Cook Quinoa:
- In a saucepan, combine quinoa and water or vegetable broth. Bring to a boil, then reduce heat to low, cover, and simmer for 15-20 minutes or until quinoa is cooked and liquid is absorbed. Fluff with a fork and set aside.

Prepare Sauce:
- In a small bowl, whisk together soy sauce, hoisin sauce, rice vinegar, and sesame oil. Set aside.

Stir-Fry Vegetables:
- Heat vegetable oil in a large wok or skillet over medium-high heat. Add minced garlic and grated ginger, sauté for about 30 seconds until fragrant.
- Add sliced bell pepper, julienned carrot, zucchini, broccoli florets, and snap peas. Stir-fry for 3-5 minutes until the vegetables are tender-crisp.

Add Tofu or Chicken (Optional):
- If using tofu or cooked chicken, add it to the wok and stir to combine with the vegetables.

Combine with Quinoa:
- Add the cooked quinoa to the wok, pour the sauce over the mixture, and toss everything together until well combined and heated through.

Adjust Seasoning:
- Taste the stir-fry and adjust the seasoning if needed, adding more soy sauce or sesame oil to your liking.

Serve:
- Garnish the Quinoa and Vegetable Stir-Fry with chopped green onions and sesame seeds.
- Serve hot and enjoy!

This Quinoa and Vegetable Stir-Fry is a versatile and nutritious dish that you can customize with your favorite vegetables and protein. It's a quick and flavorful option for a wholesome meal.

Southwest Quinoa Casserole

Ingredients:

- 1 cup quinoa, rinsed
- 2 cups vegetable broth or water
- 1 tablespoon olive oil
- 1 onion, finely chopped
- 2 cloves garlic, minced
- 1 bell pepper, diced
- 1 can (15 oz) black beans, drained and rinsed
- 1 cup corn kernels (fresh, frozen, or canned)
- 1 cup cherry tomatoes, halved
- 1 teaspoon ground cumin
- 1 teaspoon chili powder
- 1/2 teaspoon smoked paprika
- Salt and pepper to taste
- 1 cup shredded cheddar or Mexican cheese blend
- Fresh cilantro, chopped, for garnish
- Avocado slices, for serving (optional)
- Lime wedges, for serving

Instructions:

Preheat Oven:
- Preheat your oven to 375°F (190°C).

Cook Quinoa:
- In a saucepan, combine quinoa and vegetable broth or water. Bring to a boil, then reduce heat to low, cover, and simmer for 15-20 minutes or until quinoa is cooked and liquid is absorbed. Fluff with a fork and set aside.

Sauté Vegetables:
- In a large skillet, heat olive oil over medium heat. Add chopped onion and cook until softened.
- Add minced garlic and diced bell pepper. Sauté for an additional 2-3 minutes until the vegetables are tender.

Add Black Beans, Corn, and Tomatoes:
- Stir in black beans, corn kernels, and halved cherry tomatoes.

Seasoning:

- Add ground cumin, chili powder, smoked paprika, salt, and pepper. Mix well to combine.

Combine with Quinoa:
- Add the cooked quinoa to the skillet and mix everything together.

Transfer to Casserole Dish:
- Transfer the quinoa and vegetable mixture to a greased casserole dish.

Top with Cheese:
- Sprinkle shredded cheese over the top of the casserole.

Bake:
- Bake in the preheated oven for 20-25 minutes or until the cheese is melted and bubbly.

Garnish and Serve:
- Garnish the Southwest Quinoa Casserole with chopped cilantro.
- Serve hot with optional avocado slices and lime wedges on the side.

This Southwest Quinoa Casserole is a flavorful and satisfying dish that combines the goodness of quinoa with the bold flavors of the Southwest. Enjoy!

Spinach and Feta Quinoa Cakes

Ingredients:

- 1 cup quinoa, rinsed
- 2 cups vegetable broth or water
- 1 cup fresh spinach, chopped
- 1/2 cup feta cheese, crumbled
- 1/4 cup grated Parmesan cheese
- 2 green onions, finely chopped
- 2 cloves garlic, minced
- 2 large eggs
- 1/2 cup breadcrumbs
- 1 teaspoon dried oregano
- Salt and pepper to taste
- Olive oil for cooking

Instructions:

Cook Quinoa:
- In a saucepan, combine quinoa and vegetable broth or water. Bring to a boil, then reduce heat to low, cover, and simmer for 15-20 minutes or until quinoa is cooked and liquid is absorbed. Fluff with a fork and let it cool.

Prepare Spinach:
- In a large bowl, combine the chopped fresh spinach, crumbled feta cheese, grated Parmesan cheese, green onions, and minced garlic.

Mix Quinoa and Spinach Mixture:
- Add the cooled quinoa to the bowl with the spinach mixture and mix well.

Add Eggs and Breadcrumbs:
- Beat the eggs and add them to the quinoa and spinach mixture. Mix in breadcrumbs, dried oregano, salt, and pepper.

Form Quinoa Cakes:
- Shape the mixture into small patties, forming quinoa cakes.

Cook Quinoa Cakes:
- Heat olive oil in a skillet over medium heat. Add the quinoa cakes and cook for 3-4 minutes per side or until golden brown and crispy.

Serve:
- Once the quinoa cakes are cooked through and have a nice golden color, transfer them to a serving plate.

Garnish and Enjoy:
- Garnish the Spinach and Feta Quinoa Cakes with additional crumbled feta, chopped green onions, or a dollop of Greek yogurt if desired.
- Serve hot and enjoy!

These Spinach and Feta Quinoa Cakes make a delicious and nutritious appetizer or a light meal. They're packed with flavor and are a great way to enjoy the goodness of quinoa and spinach.

Quinoa Chili

Ingredients:

- 1 cup quinoa, rinsed
- 2 cups vegetable broth or water
- 1 tablespoon olive oil
- 1 onion, diced
- 3 cloves garlic, minced
- 1 bell pepper, diced
- 1 zucchini, diced
- 1 carrot, diced
- 1 can (15 oz) black beans, drained and rinsed
- 1 can (15 oz) kidney beans, drained and rinsed
- 1 can (15 oz) diced tomatoes
- 1 can (6 oz) tomato paste
- 3 cups vegetable broth
- 2 tablespoons chili powder
- 1 tablespoon cumin
- 1 teaspoon smoked paprika
- 1 teaspoon oregano
- Salt and pepper to taste
- Optional toppings: shredded cheese, chopped green onions, cilantro, sour cream

Instructions:

Cook Quinoa:
- In a saucepan, combine quinoa and 2 cups of vegetable broth or water. Bring to a boil, then reduce heat to low, cover, and simmer for 15-20 minutes or until quinoa is cooked and liquid is absorbed. Fluff with a fork and set aside.

Sauté Vegetables:
- In a large pot or Dutch oven, heat olive oil over medium heat. Add diced onion, garlic, bell pepper, zucchini, and carrot. Sauté for 5-7 minutes until the vegetables are softened.

Add Beans and Tomatoes:
- Stir in black beans, kidney beans, diced tomatoes, and tomato paste.

Add Quinoa:

- Add the cooked quinoa to the pot and mix well with the vegetables and beans.

Seasoning:
- Add chili powder, cumin, smoked paprika, oregano, salt, and pepper. Stir to combine.

Pour in Vegetable Broth:
- Pour in 3 cups of vegetable broth, bringing the chili to a simmer. Allow it to cook for at least 20-30 minutes to let the flavors meld.

Adjust Seasoning:
- Taste the chili and adjust the seasoning if needed, adding more salt, pepper, or spices according to your preference.

Serve:
- Ladle the quinoa chili into bowls and garnish with your favorite toppings such as shredded cheese, chopped green onions, cilantro, or a dollop of sour cream.

Enjoy this hearty and flavorful Quinoa Chili, a nutritious twist on a classic comfort food!

Teriyaki Salmon with Quinoa

Ingredients:

For Teriyaki Salmon:

- 4 salmon fillets
- 1/4 cup soy sauce
- 2 tablespoons honey
- 1 tablespoon rice vinegar
- 1 tablespoon mirin (sweet rice wine)
- 1 teaspoon sesame oil
- 2 cloves garlic, minced
- 1 teaspoon grated ginger
- Sesame seeds for garnish (optional)
- Green onions, chopped, for garnish (optional)

For Quinoa:

- 1 cup quinoa, rinsed
- 2 cups water or vegetable broth
- Salt to taste

For Stir-Fried Vegetables (optional):

- 1 cup broccoli florets
- 1 carrot, julienned
- 1 bell pepper, sliced
- 1 tablespoon vegetable oil
- Salt and pepper to taste

Instructions:

Prepare Quinoa:
- In a saucepan, combine quinoa and water or vegetable broth. Bring to a boil, then reduce heat to low, cover, and simmer for 15-20 minutes or until quinoa is cooked and liquid is absorbed. Fluff with a fork and set aside.

Prepare Teriyaki Marinade:
- In a bowl, whisk together soy sauce, honey, rice vinegar, mirin, sesame oil, minced garlic, and grated ginger to make the teriyaki marinade.

Marinate Salmon:
- Place the salmon fillets in a shallow dish and pour half of the teriyaki marinade over them. Let it marinate for at least 15-20 minutes.

Cook Salmon:
- Preheat the oven to 400°F (200°C).
- Place the marinated salmon on a baking sheet lined with parchment paper. Bake for 12-15 minutes or until the salmon is cooked through and flakes easily with a fork.

Prepare Quinoa and Vegetables (Optional):
- While the salmon is baking, you can stir-fry vegetables in a separate pan. Heat vegetable oil in a skillet over medium-high heat. Add broccoli, carrot, and bell pepper. Season with salt and pepper. Stir-fry for 5-7 minutes until vegetables are tender yet still crisp.

Assemble:
- Fluff the quinoa with a fork and divide it among plates.
- Top each plate with a portion of the teriyaki salmon and stir-fried vegetables (if using).

Drizzle with Remaining Teriyaki Sauce:
- Drizzle the remaining teriyaki sauce over the salmon fillets.

Garnish and Serve:
- Garnish with sesame seeds and chopped green onions if desired.
- Serve immediately and enjoy your Teriyaki Salmon with Quinoa!

This Teriyaki Salmon with Quinoa is a delicious and nutritious dish that brings together the savory flavors of teriyaki and the wholesome goodness of quinoa. Enjoy!

Barley Beauties:
Mushroom Barley Soup

Ingredients:

- 1 cup pearl barley
- 8 cups vegetable or mushroom broth
- 2 tablespoons olive oil
- 1 onion, finely chopped
- 2 carrots, diced
- 2 celery stalks, diced
- 3 cloves garlic, minced
- 1 pound (about 450g) mushrooms, sliced (use a mix of varieties like cremini, button, and shiitake)
- 1 teaspoon dried thyme
- 1 bay leaf
- Salt and pepper to taste
- Fresh parsley, chopped, for garnish

Instructions:

Prepare Barley:
- Rinse the pearl barley under cold water. In a separate pot, cook the barley according to package instructions. Drain and set aside.

Sauté Vegetables:
- In a large soup pot, heat olive oil over medium heat. Add chopped onion, diced carrots, and diced celery. Sauté for 5-7 minutes until the vegetables are softened.

Add Mushrooms and Garlic:
- Add sliced mushrooms to the pot and cook for an additional 5 minutes until the mushrooms release their moisture. Add minced garlic and cook for another 1-2 minutes.

Combine Barley and Broth:
- Stir in the cooked barley and pour in the vegetable or mushroom broth.

Seasoning:
- Add dried thyme, bay leaf, salt, and pepper. Bring the soup to a simmer.

Simmer:
- Reduce the heat to low, cover the pot, and let the soup simmer for about 30-40 minutes to allow the flavors to meld.

Adjust Seasoning:
- Taste the soup and adjust the seasoning if needed, adding more salt and pepper to your liking.

Serve:
- Ladle the Mushroom Barley Soup into bowls and garnish with chopped fresh parsley.

This Mushroom Barley Soup is comforting, hearty, and filled with the earthy flavors of mushrooms and the nutty richness of barley. Enjoy it on a chilly day for a satisfying and nourishing meal!

Barley Risotto with Asparagus and Parmesan

Ingredients:

- 1 cup pearl barley
- 1 bunch asparagus, trimmed and cut into bite-sized pieces
- 1 onion, finely chopped
- 2 cloves garlic, minced
- 1/2 cup dry white wine (optional)
- 4 cups vegetable or chicken broth, kept warm
- 1/2 cup grated Parmesan cheese
- 2 tablespoons olive oil
- Salt and pepper to taste
- Fresh parsley, chopped, for garnish

Instructions:

Prepare Asparagus:
- Blanch the asparagus in boiling water for 2-3 minutes, then transfer to an ice bath to stop the cooking process. Drain and set aside.

Sauté Onion and Garlic:
- In a large skillet or pan, heat olive oil over medium heat. Add chopped onion and sauté until softened.

Add Barley:
- Add the pearl barley to the skillet and toast it for about 2-3 minutes, stirring frequently.

Deglaze with Wine (Optional):
- Pour in the white wine (if using) to deglaze the pan. Stir until the wine has mostly evaporated.

Start Adding Broth:
- Begin adding warm broth to the barley mixture one ladle at a time. Allow the barley to absorb the liquid before adding the next ladle. Stir frequently.

Continue Cooking:
- Continue adding broth and stirring until the barley is creamy and cooked to your desired tenderness. This process usually takes about 30-40 minutes.

Add Asparagus:
- In the last 10 minutes of cooking, add the blanched asparagus to the barley mixture. Continue stirring and adding broth until the asparagus is tender and the barley is cooked.

Finish with Parmesan:
- Stir in the grated Parmesan cheese, and season with salt and pepper to taste. Continue stirring until the cheese is melted and the risotto has a creamy consistency.

Garnish and Serve:
- Garnish the Barley Risotto with chopped fresh parsley.
- Serve hot, and optionally, top with extra Parmesan.

This Barley Risotto with Asparagus and Parmesan is a flavorful and wholesome alternative to traditional rice risotto. Enjoy the nutty taste of barley combined with the freshness of asparagus and the richness of Parmesan!

Mediterranean Barley Salad

Ingredients:

- 1 cup pearl barley
- 2 1/2 cups water or vegetable broth
- 1 cucumber, diced
- 1 cup cherry tomatoes, halved
- 1/2 red onion, finely chopped
- 1/2 cup Kalamata olives, sliced
- 1/2 cup crumbled feta cheese
- 1/4 cup fresh parsley, chopped
- 1/4 cup fresh mint, chopped
- 1/4 cup extra-virgin olive oil
- 2 tablespoons red wine vinegar
- 1 clove garlic, minced
- Salt and pepper to taste
- Lemon wedges for serving

Instructions:

Cook Barley:
- Rinse the pearl barley under cold water. In a saucepan, combine barley with water or vegetable broth. Bring to a boil, then reduce heat to low, cover, and simmer for 30-40 minutes or until barley is tender. Drain any excess liquid and let it cool.

Prepare Veggies:
- In a large bowl, combine the cooled barley with diced cucumber, halved cherry tomatoes, chopped red onion, sliced Kalamata olives, crumbled feta cheese, chopped parsley, and chopped mint.

Make Dressing:
- In a small bowl, whisk together extra-virgin olive oil, red wine vinegar, minced garlic, salt, and pepper to make the dressing.

Combine and Toss:
- Pour the dressing over the barley and vegetable mixture. Toss everything together until well combined and evenly coated.

Chill and Marinate:
- Refrigerate the Mediterranean Barley Salad for at least 30 minutes to allow the flavors to meld.

Serve:
- Before serving, give the salad a final toss. Serve chilled with lemon wedges on the side.

This Mediterranean Barley Salad is not only flavorful but also packed with wholesome ingredients. It makes for a great side dish or a light and nutritious meal on its own. Enjoy the vibrant colors and fresh taste of the Mediterranean!

Beef and Barley Stew

Ingredients:

- 1.5 lbs (700g) stewing beef, cubed
- 1 cup pearl barley
- 2 tablespoons olive oil
- 1 onion, chopped
- 3 carrots, sliced
- 2 celery stalks, sliced
- 3 cloves garlic, minced
- 1 can (14 oz) diced tomatoes
- 4 cups beef broth
- 1 cup red wine (optional)
- 1 bay leaf
- 1 teaspoon dried thyme
- Salt and pepper to taste
- Fresh parsley, chopped, for garnish

Instructions:

Brown the Beef:
- In a large pot or Dutch oven, heat olive oil over medium-high heat. Add the cubed beef and brown on all sides. Remove beef from the pot and set aside.

Sauté Vegetables:
- In the same pot, add chopped onion, sliced carrots, and sliced celery. Sauté for 5-7 minutes until the vegetables are softened.

Add Garlic and Deglaze:
- Add minced garlic and sauté for an additional minute. If using red wine, pour it into the pot to deglaze, scraping up any browned bits from the bottom.

Combine Ingredients:
- Return the browned beef to the pot. Add diced tomatoes, beef broth, pearl barley, bay leaf, dried thyme, salt, and pepper.

Simmer:
- Bring the stew to a boil, then reduce the heat to low, cover, and simmer for about 1.5 to 2 hours, or until the beef is tender and the barley is cooked.

Adjust Seasoning:
- Taste the stew and adjust the seasoning if needed. Remove the bay leaf.

Serve:
- Ladle the Beef and Barley Stew into bowls, garnish with chopped fresh parsley, and serve hot.

This Beef and Barley Stew is a comforting and filling dish, perfect for colder days. The combination of tender beef, hearty barley, and savory broth creates a delicious and satisfying meal. Enjoy!

Barley and Vegetable Stir-Fry

Ingredients:

- 1 cup pearl barley, rinsed
- 2 cups water or vegetable broth
- 2 tablespoons soy sauce
- 1 tablespoon hoisin sauce
- 1 tablespoon sesame oil
- 1 tablespoon vegetable oil
- 2 cloves garlic, minced
- 1 tablespoon ginger, grated
- 1 bell pepper, thinly sliced
- 1 carrot, julienned
- 1 zucchini, sliced
- 1 cup broccoli florets
- 1 cup snap peas, trimmed
- 1 cup firm tofu, diced (optional)
- Green onions, chopped, for garnish
- Sesame seeds, for garnish

Instructions:

Cook Barley:
- In a saucepan, combine barley and water or vegetable broth. Bring to a boil, then reduce heat to low, cover, and simmer for 30-40 minutes or until barley is tender. Drain any excess liquid.

Prepare Sauce:
- In a small bowl, whisk together soy sauce, hoisin sauce, and sesame oil. Set aside.

Stir-Fry Vegetables:
- Heat vegetable oil in a wok or large skillet over medium-high heat. Add minced garlic and grated ginger, sauté for about 30 seconds until fragrant.
- Add sliced bell pepper, julienned carrot, zucchini, broccoli florets, and snap peas. Stir-fry for 5-7 minutes until the vegetables are tender-crisp.

Add Tofu (Optional):
- If using tofu, add it to the wok and stir to combine with the vegetables. Cook for an additional 2-3 minutes.

Combine Barley and Sauce:
- Add the cooked barley to the wok and pour the sauce over the mixture. Toss everything together until well combined.

Adjust Seasoning:
- Taste the stir-fry and adjust the seasoning if needed, adding more soy sauce or sesame oil to your liking.

Serve:
- Garnish the Barley and Vegetable Stir-Fry with chopped green onions and sesame seeds.
- Serve hot and enjoy your nutritious and flavorful stir-fry!

This Barley and Vegetable Stir-Fry is a wholesome and satisfying dish that's loaded with a variety of colorful vegetables and the nutty goodness of barley. It's perfect for a quick and nutritious weeknight meal.

Barley and Lentil Pilaf

Ingredients:

- 1 cup pearl barley, rinsed
- 1/2 cup green or brown lentils, rinsed
- 3 cups vegetable broth or water
- 2 tablespoons olive oil
- 1 onion, finely chopped
- 2 carrots, diced
- 2 celery stalks, diced
- 3 cloves garlic, minced
- 1 teaspoon ground cumin
- 1 teaspoon ground coriander
- 1/2 teaspoon turmeric
- 1/2 teaspoon smoked paprika
- Salt and pepper to taste
- 1/4 cup fresh parsley, chopped
- Lemon wedges for serving

Instructions:

Cook Lentils and Barley:
- In a saucepan, combine the rinsed barley, lentils, and vegetable broth or water. Bring to a boil, then reduce heat to low, cover, and simmer for 25-30 minutes or until both barley and lentils are tender. Drain any excess liquid.

Sauté Vegetables:
- In a large skillet, heat olive oil over medium heat. Add chopped onion, diced carrots, and diced celery. Sauté for 5-7 minutes until the vegetables are softened.

Add Garlic and Spices:
- Add minced garlic to the skillet and sauté for an additional 1-2 minutes until fragrant. Stir in ground cumin, ground coriander, turmeric, smoked paprika, salt, and pepper.

Combine with Barley and Lentils:
- Add the cooked barley and lentils to the skillet with the sautéed vegetables. Mix well to combine and let it cook for a few more minutes for the flavors to meld.

Adjust Seasoning:

- Taste the pilaf and adjust the seasoning if needed, adding more salt, pepper, or spices according to your preference.

Garnish and Serve:
- Garnish the Barley and Lentil Pilaf with chopped fresh parsley.
- Serve hot with lemon wedges on the side for squeezing over the pilaf.

This Barley and Lentil Pilaf is a wholesome and flavorful dish that provides a perfect balance of protein and fiber. Enjoy it as a side dish or a main course for a nutritious and satisfying meal.

Barley and Chickpea Bowl

Ingredients:

For the Barley:

- 1 cup pearl barley, rinsed
- 3 cups vegetable broth or water
- Salt to taste

For the Chickpeas:

- 1 can (15 oz) chickpeas, drained and rinsed
- 1 tablespoon olive oil
- 1 teaspoon ground cumin
- 1 teaspoon smoked paprika
- Salt and pepper to taste

For the Bowl:

- 2 cups mixed greens (e.g., spinach, kale, arugula)
- 1 cucumber, sliced
- 1 cup cherry tomatoes, halved
- 1/2 red onion, thinly sliced
- 1/4 cup feta cheese, crumbled (optional)
- 1/4 cup fresh parsley, chopped

For the Dressing:

- 3 tablespoons olive oil
- 2 tablespoons balsamic vinegar
- 1 teaspoon Dijon mustard
- Salt and pepper to taste

Instructions:

Cook Barley:
- In a saucepan, combine barley and vegetable broth or water. Bring to a boil, then reduce heat to low, cover, and simmer for 30-40 minutes or until barley is tender. Drain any excess liquid and season with salt.

Roast Chickpeas:
- Preheat the oven to 400°F (200°C). In a bowl, toss chickpeas with olive oil, ground cumin, smoked paprika, salt, and pepper. Spread them on a baking sheet and roast for 20-25 minutes or until crispy, shaking the pan occasionally.

Prepare Vegetables:
- Assemble your bowl with mixed greens, cucumber slices, cherry tomatoes, red onion slices, and any other desired vegetables.

Make Dressing:
- In a small bowl, whisk together olive oil, balsamic vinegar, Dijon mustard, salt, and pepper.

Assemble the Bowl:
- Divide the cooked barley among bowls, top with roasted chickpeas, and arrange the mixed vegetables on the side.

Drizzle with Dressing:
- Drizzle the dressing over the bowl, and if desired, sprinkle with crumbled feta cheese and chopped fresh parsley.

Serve:
- Serve the Barley and Chickpea Bowl immediately, and enjoy!

This Barley and Chickpea Bowl is not only nutritious but also full of flavor and texture. It's a versatile dish, and you can customize it with your favorite vegetables and toppings. Enjoy!

Lemon Barley Water

Ingredients:

- 1/2 cup pearl barley
- 6 cups water
- 1-2 lemons, juiced
- 1/4 cup honey or to taste
- Ice cubes (optional)
- Lemon slices and fresh mint for garnish (optional)

Instructions:

Rinse Barley:
- Rinse the pearl barley under cold water.

Boil Barley:
- In a large saucepan, combine the rinsed barley and 6 cups of water. Bring it to a boil, then reduce the heat to low, cover, and simmer for about 30-40 minutes or until the barley is cooked and the water has absorbed.

Strain Barley:
- Strain the barley from the water using a fine-mesh strainer. You can reserve the cooked barley for other dishes or discard it.

Cool Barley Water:
- Allow the barley water to cool to room temperature.

Add Lemon Juice:
- Once cooled, add the juice of 1-2 lemons to the barley water. Adjust the amount of lemon juice to your taste preference.

Sweeten with Honey:
- Stir in honey to sweeten the barley water. Adjust the sweetness according to your liking.

Chill (Optional):
- Refrigerate the lemon barley water to chill it. You can also serve it over ice cubes for an extra-refreshing drink.

Garnish (Optional):
- If desired, garnish the lemon barley water with lemon slices and fresh mint.

Serve:
- Pour the lemon barley water into glasses and serve chilled.

Lemon barley water is a hydrating and flavorful drink that can be enjoyed on its own or as a refreshing addition to your beverage options. It's a classic summer beverage with a light citrusy taste.

Barley and Roasted Butternut Squash

Ingredients:

- 1 cup pearl barley, rinsed
- 2 1/2 cups water or vegetable broth
- 1 small butternut squash, peeled, seeded, and diced
- 2 tablespoons olive oil
- 1 teaspoon ground cumin
- 1 teaspoon smoked paprika
- Salt and pepper to taste
- 1/2 cup crumbled feta cheese
- 1/4 cup fresh parsley, chopped
- 1/4 cup pepitas (pumpkin seeds), toasted (optional)

Instructions:

Preheat Oven:
- Preheat the oven to 400°F (200°C).

Roast Butternut Squash:
- Place the diced butternut squash on a baking sheet. Drizzle with olive oil, ground cumin, smoked paprika, salt, and pepper. Toss to coat the squash evenly. Roast in the preheated oven for 25-30 minutes or until the squash is tender and lightly caramelized, stirring halfway through.

Cook Barley:
- While the butternut squash is roasting, cook the barley. In a saucepan, combine rinsed barley and water or vegetable broth. Bring to a boil, then reduce heat to low, cover, and simmer for 30-40 minutes or until barley is tender. Drain any excess liquid.

Combine Barley and Squash:
- In a large bowl, combine the cooked barley and roasted butternut squash. Toss gently to mix.

Add Feta and Parsley:
- Add crumbled feta cheese and chopped fresh parsley to the barley and squash mixture. Toss again to combine.

Adjust Seasoning:
- Taste and adjust the seasoning with additional salt and pepper if needed.

Serve:

- Serve the Barley and Roasted Butternut Squash as a side dish or a light main course. Optionally, sprinkle with toasted pepitas for added crunch.

This dish combines the nutty flavor of barley with the sweet and savory notes of roasted butternut squash, creating a delicious and wholesome meal. Enjoy!

Barley and Sausage Skillet

Ingredients:

- 1 cup pearl barley, rinsed
- 2 1/2 cups water or chicken broth
- 1 pound (about 450g) Italian sausage, casings removed
- 1 tablespoon olive oil
- 1 onion, finely chopped
- 2 cloves garlic, minced
- 1 bell pepper, diced
- 1 zucchini, diced
- 1 can (14 oz) diced tomatoes, undrained
- 1 teaspoon dried oregano
- 1 teaspoon dried thyme
- Salt and pepper to taste
- 1/2 cup grated Parmesan cheese
- Fresh parsley, chopped, for garnish

Instructions:

Cook Barley:
- In a saucepan, combine rinsed barley and water or chicken broth. Bring to a boil, then reduce heat to low, cover, and simmer for 30-40 minutes or until barley is tender. Drain any excess liquid.

Cook Sausage:
- While the barley is cooking, heat olive oil in a large skillet over medium-high heat. Add the sausage, breaking it into crumbles with a spoon. Cook until browned and cooked through. Remove excess fat if necessary.

Sauté Vegetables:
- Add chopped onion, minced garlic, diced bell pepper, and diced zucchini to the skillet. Sauté for 5-7 minutes until the vegetables are softened.

Combine Ingredients:
- Stir in the cooked barley, diced tomatoes (with their juice), dried oregano, dried thyme, salt, and pepper. Mix everything well.

Simmer:
- Let the mixture simmer for an additional 10-15 minutes to allow the flavors to meld and the ingredients to heat through.

Add Parmesan:
- Just before serving, stir in the grated Parmesan cheese until melted and well combined.

Garnish and Serve:
- Garnish the Barley and Sausage Skillet with chopped fresh parsley.
- Serve hot, and enjoy your delicious and hearty skillet meal!

This Barley and Sausage Skillet is a savory and satisfying dish that combines the richness of sausage with the wholesome goodness of barley and vegetables. It makes for a comforting and flavorful dinner option.

Couscous Concoctions:
Lemon Herb Couscous

Ingredients:

- 1 cup couscous
- 1 1/4 cups vegetable or chicken broth
- Zest of 1 lemon
- Juice of 1 lemon
- 2 tablespoons olive oil
- 2 tablespoons fresh parsley, chopped
- 1 tablespoon fresh mint, chopped
- Salt and pepper to taste

Instructions:

Prepare Couscous:
- In a saucepan, bring the vegetable or chicken broth to a boil. Stir in the couscous, cover the pot with a lid, and remove it from the heat. Let it sit for 5 minutes to allow the couscous to absorb the liquid.

Fluff Couscous:
- After 5 minutes, uncover the pot and fluff the couscous with a fork to separate the grains.

Add Lemon Zest and Juice:
- Add the lemon zest and lemon juice to the couscous. Stir well to distribute the citrus flavor evenly.

Add Olive Oil and Herbs:
- Drizzle olive oil over the couscous and add chopped fresh parsley and mint. Gently toss the couscous to combine all the ingredients.

Season:
- Season the Lemon Herb Couscous with salt and pepper to taste. Adjust the seasoning according to your preference.

Serve:
- Serve the Lemon Herb Couscous as a side dish alongside your favorite main course. It pairs well with grilled chicken, fish, or roasted vegetables.

This Lemon Herb Couscous is light, fresh, and bursting with citrusy and herby flavors. It makes a versatile and quick side dish that complements a variety of main dishes. Enjoy!

Mediterranean Couscous Salad

Ingredients:

For the Salad:

- 1 cup couscous
- 1 1/4 cups vegetable broth or water
- 1 cup cherry tomatoes, halved
- 1 cucumber, diced
- 1/2 red onion, finely chopped
- 1/2 cup Kalamata olives, sliced
- 1/2 cup feta cheese, crumbled
- 1/4 cup fresh parsley, chopped
- 1/4 cup fresh mint, chopped

For the Dressing:

- 1/4 cup extra-virgin olive oil
- 2 tablespoons red wine vinegar
- 1 clove garlic, minced
- 1 teaspoon dried oregano
- Salt and pepper to taste

Instructions:

Cook Couscous:
- In a saucepan, bring the vegetable broth or water to a boil. Stir in the couscous, cover, and remove from heat. Let it sit for 5 minutes, then fluff the couscous with a fork to separate the grains.

Prepare Dressing:
- In a small bowl, whisk together olive oil, red wine vinegar, minced garlic, dried oregano, salt, and pepper to make the dressing.

Assemble Salad:
- In a large bowl, combine the cooked and cooled couscous with cherry tomatoes, diced cucumber, chopped red onion, sliced Kalamata olives, crumbled feta cheese, chopped fresh parsley, and chopped fresh mint.

Add Dressing:
- Pour the dressing over the couscous and vegetables. Toss everything gently to coat the salad with the dressing.

Chill (Optional):
- Refrigerate the Mediterranean Couscous Salad for at least 30 minutes before serving to allow the flavors to meld.

Serve:
- Serve the salad chilled, and enjoy as a refreshing side dish or a light and satisfying main course.

This Mediterranean Couscous Salad is a colorful and flavorful dish that showcases the vibrant tastes of the Mediterranean. It's perfect for a summer lunch, picnic, or as a side for grilled meats. Enjoy!

Couscous-stuffed Peppers

Ingredients:

- 4 large bell peppers, halved and seeds removed
- 1 cup couscous
- 2 cups vegetable broth or water
- 1 tablespoon olive oil
- 1 onion, finely chopped
- 2 cloves garlic, minced
- 1 zucchini, diced
- 1 carrot, grated
- 1 can (14 oz) diced tomatoes, drained
- 1 teaspoon ground cumin
- 1 teaspoon ground coriander
- Salt and pepper to taste
- 1/2 cup feta cheese, crumbled
- Fresh parsley, chopped, for garnish

Instructions:

Preheat Oven:
- Preheat the oven to 375°F (190°C).

Prepare Peppers:
- Cut the bell peppers in half lengthwise and remove the seeds and membranes. Place them in a baking dish.

Cook Couscous:
- In a saucepan, bring vegetable broth or water to a boil. Stir in couscous, cover, and remove from heat. Let it sit for 5 minutes, then fluff with a fork.

Sauté Vegetables:
- In a large skillet, heat olive oil over medium heat. Add chopped onion, minced garlic, diced zucchini, and grated carrot. Sauté for 5-7 minutes until the vegetables are softened.

Combine Ingredients:
- Add the cooked couscous, drained diced tomatoes, ground cumin, ground coriander, salt, and pepper to the skillet. Stir well to combine all the ingredients.

Stuff Peppers:

- Spoon the couscous mixture into each bell pepper half, pressing down gently.

Bake:
- Cover the baking dish with aluminum foil and bake in the preheated oven for 25-30 minutes or until the peppers are tender.

Add Feta and Garnish:
- Remove the foil, sprinkle crumbled feta cheese over the stuffed peppers, and bake for an additional 5-7 minutes or until the cheese is melted and bubbly.

Garnish and Serve:
- Garnish the Couscous-Stuffed Peppers with chopped fresh parsley before serving.

These Couscous-Stuffed Peppers make for a wholesome and satisfying vegetarian meal. They are packed with flavorful couscous and a variety of vegetables, creating a colorful and delicious dish. Enjoy!

Shrimp and Vegetable Couscous

Ingredients:

- 1 cup couscous
- 1 1/4 cups vegetable broth or water
- 1 tablespoon olive oil
- 1 pound (about 450g) shrimp, peeled and deveined
- 1 onion, finely chopped
- 2 bell peppers (any color), diced
- 1 zucchini, diced
- 2 cloves garlic, minced
- 1 teaspoon ground cumin
- 1 teaspoon paprika
- Salt and pepper to taste
- 1 cup cherry tomatoes, halved
- Juice of 1 lemon
- Fresh parsley, chopped, for garnish

Instructions:

Cook Couscous:
- In a saucepan, bring vegetable broth or water to a boil. Stir in couscous, cover, and remove from heat. Let it sit for 5 minutes, then fluff with a fork.

Sauté Shrimp:
- In a large skillet, heat olive oil over medium-high heat. Add shrimp and cook for 2-3 minutes per side until they are pink and opaque. Remove the shrimp from the skillet and set aside.

Sauté Vegetables:
- In the same skillet, add chopped onion, diced bell peppers, diced zucchini, and minced garlic. Sauté for 5-7 minutes until the vegetables are tender.

Season:
- Sprinkle ground cumin, paprika, salt, and pepper over the vegetables. Stir to coat evenly.

Combine Ingredients:
- Add the cooked couscous and halved cherry tomatoes to the skillet. Stir to combine the ingredients.

Add Shrimp and Lemon Juice:

- Gently fold in the cooked shrimp and squeeze the juice of one lemon over the mixture. Toss everything together to incorporate the flavors.

Adjust Seasoning:
- Taste and adjust the seasoning, adding more salt, pepper, or lemon juice if needed.

Garnish and Serve:
- Garnish the Shrimp and Vegetable Couscous with chopped fresh parsley before serving.

This Shrimp and Vegetable Couscous is a quick and flavorful dish that combines succulent shrimp with a medley of colorful vegetables and fluffy couscous. It makes for a delightful and wholesome meal. Enjoy!

Moroccan Spiced Chicken with Couscous

Ingredients:

For the Chicken:

- 4 boneless, skinless chicken breasts
- 2 teaspoons ground cumin
- 2 teaspoons ground coriander
- 1 teaspoon smoked paprika
- 1 teaspoon ground cinnamon
- 1 teaspoon ground turmeric
- Salt and pepper to taste
- 2 tablespoons olive oil

For the Couscous:

- 1 cup couscous
- 1 1/4 cups chicken broth
- Zest of 1 lemon
- 1/4 cup raisins or chopped dried apricots
- 1/4 cup chopped almonds or slivered almonds, toasted
- Fresh cilantro or parsley, chopped, for garnish

For the Yogurt Sauce:

- 1/2 cup Greek yogurt
- 1 tablespoon fresh lemon juice
- 1 tablespoon fresh mint, chopped
- Salt and pepper to taste

Instructions:

Prepare Chicken:
- In a small bowl, mix together cumin, coriander, smoked paprika, cinnamon, turmeric, salt, and pepper. Rub the spice mixture over both sides of the chicken breasts.

Cook Chicken:

- Heat olive oil in a large skillet over medium-high heat. Add the seasoned chicken breasts and cook for about 5-7 minutes per side or until fully cooked and browned. Remove from the skillet and let them rest.

Prepare Couscous:
- In a saucepan, bring chicken broth to a boil. Stir in couscous, cover, and remove from heat. Let it sit for 5 minutes, then fluff with a fork. Stir in lemon zest, raisins or chopped dried apricots, and toasted almonds.

Make Yogurt Sauce:
- In a small bowl, whisk together Greek yogurt, fresh lemon juice, chopped fresh mint, salt, and pepper to make the yogurt sauce.

Serve:
- Serve the Moroccan Spiced Chicken on a bed of couscous. Drizzle with yogurt sauce and garnish with chopped cilantro or parsley.

This Moroccan Spiced Chicken with Couscous is a flavorful and aromatic dish that brings the exotic taste of Moroccan cuisine to your table. Enjoy the combination of spices, couscous, and the refreshing yogurt sauce!

Greek-Style Couscous with Tomatoes and Feta

Ingredients:

- 1 cup couscous
- 1 1/4 cups vegetable broth or water
- 2 tablespoons olive oil
- 1 onion, finely chopped
- 2 cloves garlic, minced
- 1 can (14 oz) diced tomatoes, undrained
- 1 teaspoon dried oregano
- 1 teaspoon dried basil
- Salt and pepper to taste
- 1 cup cherry tomatoes, halved
- 1/2 cup Kalamata olives, sliced
- 1/2 cup crumbled feta cheese
- Fresh parsley, chopped, for garnish
- Lemon wedges for serving (optional)

Instructions:

Cook Couscous:
- In a saucepan, bring vegetable broth or water to a boil. Stir in couscous, cover, and remove from heat. Let it sit for 5 minutes, then fluff with a fork.

Sauté Onions and Garlic:
- In a large skillet, heat olive oil over medium heat. Add chopped onion and sauté until softened. Add minced garlic and cook for an additional 1-2 minutes until fragrant.

Add Canned Tomatoes and Seasonings:
- Pour in the can of diced tomatoes with their juice into the skillet. Stir in dried oregano, dried basil, salt, and pepper. Simmer for 10-15 minutes, allowing the flavors to meld.

Combine with Couscous:
- Add the cooked couscous to the skillet with the tomato mixture. Mix well to combine.

Add Fresh Ingredients:
- Gently fold in halved cherry tomatoes, sliced Kalamata olives, and crumbled feta cheese. Cook for an additional 2-3 minutes until the mixture is heated through.

Adjust Seasoning:
- Taste and adjust the seasoning, adding more salt or pepper if needed.

Garnish and Serve:
- Garnish the Greek-Style Couscous with chopped fresh parsley. Optionally, serve with lemon wedges on the side for squeezing over the dish.

This Greek-inspired couscous dish is a flavorful combination of Mediterranean ingredients. It's light, refreshing, and makes for a delightful side dish or a light main course. Enjoy!

Couscous with Roasted Vegetables

Ingredients:

For the Roasted Vegetables:

- 2 bell peppers (any color), sliced
- 1 zucchini, sliced
- 1 eggplant, diced
- 1 red onion, sliced
- 2 tablespoons olive oil
- 1 teaspoon dried thyme
- Salt and pepper to taste

For the Couscous:

- 1 cup couscous
- 1 1/4 cups vegetable broth or water
- 2 tablespoons olive oil
- 2 tablespoons lemon juice
- Zest of 1 lemon
- Salt and pepper to taste

Optional Garnishes:

- Fresh parsley, chopped
- Feta cheese, crumbled

Instructions:

Preheat Oven:
- Preheat the oven to 425°F (220°C).

Roast Vegetables:
- In a large bowl, toss the sliced bell peppers, zucchini, diced eggplant, and sliced red onion with olive oil, dried thyme, salt, and pepper. Spread the vegetables on a baking sheet in a single layer. Roast in the preheated oven for 25-30 minutes or until the vegetables are tender and slightly caramelized, stirring halfway through.

Cook Couscous:

- In a saucepan, bring vegetable broth or water to a boil. Stir in couscous, cover, and remove from heat. Let it sit for 5 minutes, then fluff with a fork.

Prepare Dressing:
- In a small bowl, whisk together olive oil, lemon juice, lemon zest, salt, and pepper.

Combine Ingredients:
- In a large bowl, combine the cooked couscous and roasted vegetables. Pour the dressing over the mixture and toss to coat evenly.

Adjust Seasoning:
- Taste and adjust the seasoning, adding more salt, pepper, or lemon juice if needed.

Garnish and Serve:
- Garnish the Couscous with Roasted Vegetables with chopped fresh parsley and crumbled feta cheese if desired.

Serve:
- Serve warm as a side dish or a light and satisfying main course.

This Couscous with Roasted Vegetables is a flavorful and hearty dish that showcases the sweetness of roasted vegetables combined with the lightness of couscous. Enjoy!

Harissa Chickpea Couscous

Ingredients:

- 1 cup couscous
- 1 1/4 cups vegetable broth or water
- 2 tablespoons olive oil
- 1 can (15 oz) chickpeas, drained and rinsed
- 2 tablespoons harissa paste (adjust to taste)
- 1 teaspoon ground cumin
- 1 teaspoon ground coriander
- 1 teaspoon smoked paprika
- Salt and pepper to taste
- 1 cup cherry tomatoes, halved
- 1 cucumber, diced
- 1/4 cup fresh cilantro, chopped
- 1/4 cup feta cheese, crumbled (optional)
- Lemon wedges for serving

Instructions:

Cook Couscous:
- In a saucepan, bring vegetable broth or water to a boil. Stir in couscous, cover, and remove from heat. Let it sit for 5 minutes, then fluff with a fork.

Prepare Chickpeas:
- In a large skillet, heat olive oil over medium heat. Add chickpeas, harissa paste, ground cumin, ground coriander, smoked paprika, salt, and pepper. Sauté for 5-7 minutes, stirring occasionally, until the chickpeas are coated with the spices and heated through.

Combine Ingredients:
- In a large bowl, combine the cooked couscous, spiced chickpeas, halved cherry tomatoes, diced cucumber, and chopped cilantro. Toss to mix everything evenly.

Adjust Seasoning:
- Taste and adjust the seasoning, adding more harissa, salt, or pepper if desired.

Garnish and Serve:

- Garnish the Harissa Chickpea Couscous with crumbled feta cheese (if using) and serve with lemon wedges on the side.

This Harissa Chickpea Couscous is a quick and flavorful dish with a spicy kick from the harissa. It's a perfect balance of protein, grains, and vegetables, making it a delicious and satisfying meal. Enjoy!

Couscous Tabbouleh

Ingredients:

For the Couscous:

- 1 cup couscous
- 1 1/4 cups vegetable broth or water
- 2 tablespoons olive oil
- Salt to taste

For the Tabbouleh:

- 1 cup cherry tomatoes, finely chopped
- 1 cucumber, finely diced
- 1 bunch fresh parsley, finely chopped
- 1/2 cup fresh mint, finely chopped
- 1/4 cup red onion, finely chopped
- 1/4 cup extra-virgin olive oil
- Juice of 1-2 lemons (adjust to taste)
- Salt and pepper to taste

Instructions:

Cook Couscous:
- In a saucepan, bring vegetable broth or water to a boil. Stir in couscous, cover, and remove from heat. Let it sit for 5 minutes, then fluff with a fork. Stir in olive oil and salt.

Prepare Tabbouleh:
- In a large mixing bowl, combine the cooked couscous with chopped cherry tomatoes, diced cucumber, finely chopped parsley, mint, and red onion.

Make Dressing:
- In a small bowl, whisk together extra-virgin olive oil, lemon juice, salt, and pepper to make the dressing.

Combine Ingredients:
- Pour the dressing over the couscous and vegetable mixture. Toss everything together until well combined.

Chill (Optional):
- Refrigerate the Couscous Tabbouleh for at least 30 minutes to allow the flavors to meld. This step is optional but enhances the taste.

Adjust Seasoning:
- Before serving, taste and adjust the seasoning, adding more salt, pepper, or lemon juice if needed.

Serve:
- Serve the Couscous Tabbouleh as a refreshing side dish or a light and healthy main course.

This Couscous Tabbouleh is a modern twist on the classic tabbouleh, incorporating couscous for added texture and heartiness. It's a perfect dish for a light lunch or as a side for grilled meats. Enjoy!

Spicy Sausage and Spinach Couscous

Ingredients:

- 1 cup couscous
- 1 1/4 cups chicken broth or water
- 2 tablespoons olive oil
- 1 pound (about 450g) spicy sausage, casing removed and crumbled
- 1 onion, finely chopped
- 2 cloves garlic, minced
- 1 teaspoon ground cumin
- 1 teaspoon smoked paprika
- 1/2 teaspoon red pepper flakes (adjust to taste)
- Salt and pepper to taste
- 4 cups fresh spinach, chopped
- 1/2 cup sun-dried tomatoes, chopped
- 1/4 cup grated Parmesan cheese (optional)
- Lemon wedges for serving

Instructions:

Cook Couscous:
- In a saucepan, bring chicken broth or water to a boil. Stir in couscous, cover, and remove from heat. Let it sit for 5 minutes, then fluff with a fork. Stir in 1 tablespoon of olive oil.

Sauté Sausage:
- In a large skillet, heat the remaining 1 tablespoon of olive oil over medium-high heat. Add crumbled spicy sausage and cook until browned, breaking it into smaller pieces with a spoon.

Add Aromatics and Spices:
- Add chopped onion and minced garlic to the skillet with the sausage. Sauté for 2-3 minutes until the onion is softened. Stir in ground cumin, smoked paprika, red pepper flakes, salt, and pepper.

Add Spinach and Sun-Dried Tomatoes:
- Add chopped spinach and sun-dried tomatoes to the skillet. Cook for an additional 2-3 minutes until the spinach wilts and the tomatoes are heated through.

Combine with Couscous:

- Add the cooked couscous to the skillet with the sausage and vegetables. Toss everything together until well combined.

Optional Parmesan:
- If desired, sprinkle grated Parmesan cheese over the couscous mixture and toss again.

Serve:
- Serve the Spicy Sausage and Spinach Couscous with lemon wedges on the side for squeezing over the dish.

This Spicy Sausage and Spinach Couscous is a hearty and flavorful one-pan dish. The combination of spicy sausage, fresh spinach, and sun-dried tomatoes creates a satisfying meal with a kick. Enjoy!

Wild Rice Wonders:
Wild Rice Pilaf with Cranberries and Almonds

Ingredients:

- 1 cup wild rice
- 2 1/2 cups vegetable broth or water
- 2 tablespoons olive oil
- 1 onion, finely chopped
- 2 cloves garlic, minced
- 1/2 cup sliced almonds, toasted
- 1/2 cup dried cranberries
- 1 teaspoon dried thyme
- Salt and pepper to taste
- Fresh parsley, chopped, for garnish (optional)

Instructions:

Cook Wild Rice:
- Rinse the wild rice under cold water. In a saucepan, combine the wild rice and vegetable broth or water. Bring to a boil, then reduce the heat to low, cover, and simmer for 45-55 minutes or until the rice is tender and has absorbed the liquid. Drain any excess liquid.

Sauté Aromatics:
- In a large skillet, heat olive oil over medium heat. Add chopped onion and sauté until softened. Add minced garlic and cook for an additional 1-2 minutes until fragrant.

Combine Ingredients:
- Add the cooked wild rice to the skillet with the sautéed onion and garlic. Stir in toasted sliced almonds, dried cranberries, dried thyme, salt, and pepper. Toss everything together until well combined.

Adjust Seasoning:
- Taste and adjust the seasoning, adding more salt or pepper if needed.

Garnish and Serve:
- Garnish the Wild Rice Pilaf with Cranberries and Almonds with chopped fresh parsley if desired.

Serve:
- Serve the pilaf as a delicious side dish or a light and flavorful main course.

This Wild Rice Pilaf with Cranberries and Almonds is a festive and nutritious dish with a perfect balance of flavors and textures. Enjoy the combination of hearty wild rice, sweet cranberries, and crunchy almonds!

Chicken and Wild Rice Soup

Ingredients:

- 1 cup wild rice
- 8 cups chicken broth
- 1 pound boneless, skinless chicken breasts, cooked and shredded
- 2 tablespoons olive oil
- 1 onion, finely chopped
- 3 carrots, diced
- 3 celery stalks, diced
- 3 cloves garlic, minced
- 1 teaspoon dried thyme
- 1 teaspoon dried rosemary
- Salt and pepper to taste
- 1/2 cup all-purpose flour
- 4 cups milk (whole or 2%)
- 1/2 cup heavy cream (optional)
- Fresh parsley, chopped, for garnish

Instructions:

Cook Wild Rice:
- Cook the wild rice according to the package instructions. If possible, cook it in chicken broth for added flavor. Set aside.

Sauté Vegetables:
- In a large pot, heat olive oil over medium heat. Add chopped onion, diced carrots, diced celery, and minced garlic. Sauté for 5-7 minutes until the vegetables are softened.

Add Seasonings:
- Stir in dried thyme, dried rosemary, salt, and pepper. Cook for an additional 2 minutes to allow the flavors to meld.

Make Roux:
- Sprinkle flour over the vegetable mixture and stir to create a roux. Cook for 2-3 minutes to eliminate the raw flour taste.

Add Broth and Milk:
- Gradually pour in chicken broth while stirring to avoid lumps. Add the cooked and shredded chicken. Bring the mixture to a simmer. Then, add milk and continue to simmer for 10-15 minutes, stirring occasionally.

Add Cooked Wild Rice:
- Stir in the cooked wild rice. If using heavy cream, add it at this stage. Allow the soup to simmer for an additional 10-15 minutes.

Adjust Seasoning:
- Taste and adjust the seasoning, adding more salt or pepper if needed.

Serve:
- Ladle the Chicken and Wild Rice Soup into bowls. Garnish with chopped fresh parsley and serve warm.

This Chicken and Wild Rice Soup is hearty, flavorful, and perfect for warming up on chilly days. Enjoy the comforting combination of chicken, wild rice, and aromatic herbs!

Mushroom and Spinach Stuffed Acorn Squash with Wild Rice

Ingredients:

- 2 acorn squash, halved and seeds removed
- 1 cup wild rice
- 2 1/2 cups vegetable broth or water
- 3 tablespoons olive oil, divided
- 1 onion, finely chopped
- 2 cloves garlic, minced
- 8 ounces mushrooms, finely chopped
- 4 cups fresh spinach, chopped
- 1/2 teaspoon dried thyme
- Salt and pepper to taste
- 1/2 cup grated Parmesan cheese (optional)
- 1/4 cup chopped fresh parsley, for garnish

Instructions:

Preheat Oven:
- Preheat the oven to 375°F (190°C).

Roast Acorn Squash:
- Place the halved acorn squash on a baking sheet, cut side up. Drizzle with 1 tablespoon of olive oil and season with salt and pepper. Roast in the preheated oven for about 40-45 minutes or until the squash is tender.

Cook Wild Rice:
- Rinse the wild rice under cold water. In a saucepan, bring vegetable broth or water to a boil. Stir in the wild rice, cover, and simmer for 45-55 minutes or until the rice is tender and has absorbed the liquid. Drain any excess liquid.

Sauté Vegetables:
- In a large skillet, heat the remaining 2 tablespoons of olive oil over medium heat. Add chopped onion and sauté until softened. Add minced garlic, chopped mushrooms, and cook until the mushrooms release their moisture and become golden brown. Stir in chopped spinach, dried thyme, salt, and pepper. Cook until the spinach is wilted.

Combine Ingredients:

- In a large mixing bowl, combine the cooked wild rice with the sautéed mushroom and spinach mixture. Optionally, stir in grated Parmesan cheese.

Stuff Acorn Squash:
- Stuff each roasted acorn squash half with the wild rice, mushroom, and spinach mixture.

Bake:
- Place the stuffed acorn squash back in the oven and bake for an additional 15-20 minutes or until heated through.

Garnish and Serve:
- Garnish the Mushroom and Spinach Stuffed Acorn Squash with chopped fresh parsley before serving.

This dish combines the earthy flavors of mushrooms and spinach with the nuttiness of wild rice, all nestled in the sweet and tender roasted acorn squash. It makes for a satisfying and visually appealing meal. Enjoy!

Wild Rice and Turkey Meatballs

Ingredients:

For the Turkey Meatballs:

- 1 pound ground turkey
- 1 cup cooked wild rice
- 1/2 cup breadcrumbs
- 1/4 cup grated Parmesan cheese
- 1/4 cup finely chopped onion
- 2 cloves garlic, minced
- 1 teaspoon dried oregano
- 1 teaspoon dried basil
- Salt and pepper to taste
- 1 large egg, beaten
- Olive oil for cooking

For the Sauce:

- 1 can (14 oz) crushed tomatoes
- 1 clove garlic, minced
- 1 teaspoon dried Italian seasoning
- Salt and pepper to taste

For Serving:

- Cooked pasta or rice
- Fresh basil or parsley, chopped (optional)

Instructions:

Preheat Oven:
- Preheat the oven to 400°F (200°C).

Make Turkey Meatballs:

- In a large bowl, combine ground turkey, cooked wild rice, breadcrumbs, grated Parmesan cheese, chopped onion, minced garlic, dried oregano, dried basil, salt, pepper, and beaten egg. Mix until well combined.

Shape Meatballs:
- Form the mixture into meatballs, about 1 to 1.5 inches in diameter. Place them on a baking sheet lined with parchment paper.

Bake Meatballs:
- Bake in the preheated oven for 20-25 minutes or until the meatballs are cooked through and browned on the outside.

Prepare Sauce:
- While the meatballs are baking, prepare the sauce. In a saucepan, combine crushed tomatoes, minced garlic, dried Italian seasoning, salt, and pepper. Simmer over low heat for about 15 minutes, stirring occasionally.

Combine Meatballs and Sauce:
- Once the meatballs are done, add them to the tomato sauce. Allow them to simmer in the sauce for an additional 5-10 minutes to absorb the flavors.

Serve:
- Serve the Wild Rice and Turkey Meatballs over cooked pasta or rice. Garnish with chopped fresh basil or parsley if desired.

This dish combines the lean and flavorful turkey meatballs with the nuttiness of wild rice, all coated in a savory tomato sauce. It's a wholesome and satisfying meal that's perfect for dinner. Enjoy!

Wild Rice and Roasted Vegetable Salad

Ingredients:

For the Salad:

- 1 cup wild rice
- 2 1/2 cups vegetable broth or water
- 1 sweet potato, peeled and diced
- 1 red bell pepper, diced
- 1 zucchini, diced
- 1 red onion, thinly sliced
- 2 tablespoons olive oil
- Salt and pepper to taste
- 1/2 cup feta cheese, crumbled
- 1/4 cup fresh parsley, chopped

For the Dressing:

- 3 tablespoons olive oil
- 2 tablespoons balsamic vinegar
- 1 tablespoon Dijon mustard
- 1 clove garlic, minced
- Salt and pepper to taste

Instructions:

Cook Wild Rice:
- Rinse the wild rice under cold water. In a saucepan, bring vegetable broth or water to a boil. Stir in the wild rice, cover, and simmer for 45-55 minutes or until the rice is tender and has absorbed the liquid. Drain any excess liquid.

Roast Vegetables:
- Preheat the oven to 400°F (200°C). Place the diced sweet potato, red bell pepper, zucchini, and red onion on a baking sheet. Drizzle with 2 tablespoons of olive oil and season with salt and pepper. Toss to coat the vegetables evenly. Roast in the preheated oven for about 25-30 minutes or

until the vegetables are tender and slightly caramelized, stirring halfway through.

Prepare Dressing:
- In a small bowl, whisk together 3 tablespoons of olive oil, balsamic vinegar, Dijon mustard, minced garlic, salt, and pepper to make the dressing.

Combine Ingredients:
- In a large mixing bowl, combine the cooked wild rice, roasted vegetables, crumbled feta cheese, and chopped fresh parsley.

Add Dressing:
- Pour the dressing over the salad and toss everything together until well coated.

Serve:
- Serve the Wild Rice and Roasted Vegetable Salad at room temperature or chilled. It can be served as a side dish or a light and satisfying main course.

This salad brings together the nutty flavor of wild rice with the sweetness of roasted vegetables and the tanginess of the balsamic dressing. It's a nutritious and flavorful dish that's perfect for any occasion. Enjoy!

Creamy Wild Mushroom RIsotto with Truffle Oil

Ingredients:

- 1 cup Arborio rice
- 1/2 cup dry white wine
- 4 cups chicken or vegetable broth, kept warm
- 2 tablespoons olive oil
- 1/2 cup shallots, finely chopped
- 2 cloves garlic, minced
- 1 cup mixed wild mushrooms (such as shiitake, oyster, and cremini), sliced
- 1/2 cup Parmesan cheese, grated
- 2 tablespoons unsalted butter
- Salt and pepper to taste
- Truffle oil for drizzling
- Fresh parsley, chopped, for garnish

Instructions:

Sauté Mushrooms:
- In a large skillet or pan, heat 1 tablespoon of olive oil over medium heat. Add the chopped shallots and garlic, sauté until softened.

Add Rice:
- Stir in Arborio rice and cook for 1-2 minutes until the rice is lightly toasted.

Deglaze with Wine:
- Pour in the dry white wine and stir constantly until the wine is mostly absorbed by the rice.

Cook the Mushrooms:
- In the same pan, add the sliced wild mushrooms and cook until they are tender and any liquid they release is evaporated.

Begin Risotto Cooking:
- Begin adding the warm broth, one ladle at a time, stirring frequently. Wait until most of the liquid is absorbed before adding the next ladle of broth. Continue this process until the rice is creamy and cooked to al dente texture. This should take about 18-20 minutes.

Finish and Season:
- Once the rice is cooked, stir in the grated Parmesan cheese and butter. Season with salt and pepper to taste. The risotto should have a creamy consistency.

Drizzle with Truffle Oil:
- Drizzle truffle oil over the risotto and gently stir to incorporate the truffle flavor.

Garnish and Serve:
- Garnish the Creamy Wild Mushroom Risotto with chopped fresh parsley. Serve immediately.

This Creamy Wild Mushroom Risotto with Truffle Oil is a rich and indulgent dish, perfect for special occasions or when you want to treat yourself to a comforting meal. Enjoy the luxurious flavors!

Wild Rice and Quinoa Cakes

Ingredients:

- 1/2 cup wild rice, cooked
- 1/2 cup quinoa, cooked
- 1/2 cup breadcrumbs
- 1/4 cup grated Parmesan cheese
- 1/4 cup red bell pepper, finely chopped
- 2 green onions, finely chopped
- 2 cloves garlic, minced
- 1 teaspoon dried thyme
- 1 teaspoon dried oregano
- Salt and pepper to taste
- 2 large eggs, beaten
- Olive oil for cooking

For Serving:

- Greek yogurt or sour cream
- Fresh herbs for garnish (such as parsley or chives)

Instructions:

Cook Wild Rice and Quinoa:
- Cook wild rice and quinoa separately according to package instructions. Allow them to cool.

Prepare the Mixture:
- In a large mixing bowl, combine the cooked wild rice, cooked quinoa, breadcrumbs, grated Parmesan cheese, chopped red bell pepper, green onions, minced garlic, dried thyme, dried oregano, salt, and pepper. Mix well.

Add Eggs:
- Stir in the beaten eggs, ensuring that the mixture is well combined.

Shape into Cakes:
- Take a portion of the mixture and shape it into a round, flat cake. Repeat until all the mixture is used.

Cook the Cakes:

- Heat olive oil in a skillet over medium heat. Place the shaped wild rice and quinoa cakes in the skillet and cook until they are golden brown on each side, approximately 3-4 minutes per side.

Serve:
- Once the cakes are cooked through and crispy on the outside, transfer them to a serving plate.

Garnish and Serve:
- Serve the Wild Rice and Quinoa Cakes with a dollop of Greek yogurt or sour cream. Garnish with fresh herbs like parsley or chives.

These Wild Rice and Quinoa Cakes make a delightful and nutritious dish. They can be served as a vegetarian main course or a tasty side dish. Enjoy the flavorful combination of wild rice, quinoa, and herbs!

Orange Pecan Wild Rice

Ingredients:

- 1 cup wild rice
- 2 1/2 cups vegetable or chicken broth
- Zest of 1 orange
- 1/2 cup fresh orange juice
- 1/2 cup chopped pecans, toasted
- 2 tablespoons butter
- Salt and pepper to taste
- Fresh parsley, chopped, for garnish (optional)
- Orange slices for garnish (optional)

Instructions:

Cook Wild Rice:
- Rinse the wild rice under cold water. In a saucepan, bring vegetable or chicken broth to a boil. Stir in the wild rice, cover, and simmer for 45-55 minutes or until the rice is tender and has absorbed the liquid. Drain any excess liquid.

Prepare Orange Pecan Mixture:
- In a separate bowl, mix together the orange zest, fresh orange juice, and chopped toasted pecans.

Combine Ingredients:
- In a large skillet, melt the butter over medium heat. Add the cooked wild rice to the skillet and pour the orange pecan mixture over it. Toss everything together until well combined.

Season:
- Season the Orange Pecan Wild Rice with salt and pepper to taste. Adjust the seasoning as needed.

Garnish and Serve:
- Garnish with chopped fresh parsley and orange slices if desired. Serve warm.

This Orange Pecan Wild Rice is a flavorful side dish that pairs well with a variety of proteins, such as poultry or fish. The combination of citrusy orange and crunchy pecans adds a delightful twist to the nutty wild rice. Enjoy!

Lemon Garlic Shrimp with Wild Rice

Ingredients:

For the Lemon Garlic Shrimp:

- 1 pound large shrimp, peeled and deveined
- 3 tablespoons olive oil
- 4 cloves garlic, minced
- Zest of 1 lemon
- Juice of 1 lemon
- 1 teaspoon dried oregano
- Salt and pepper to taste
- Crushed red pepper flakes (optional, for heat)
- Fresh parsley, chopped, for garnish

For the Wild Rice:

- 1 cup wild rice
- 2 1/2 cups chicken or vegetable broth
- 1 tablespoon butter (optional)
- Salt to taste

Instructions:

Cook Wild Rice:
- Rinse the wild rice under cold water. In a saucepan, bring chicken or vegetable broth to a boil. Stir in the wild rice, cover, and simmer for 45-55 minutes or until the rice is tender and has absorbed the liquid. Drain any excess liquid. Stir in butter and salt to taste.

Prepare Lemon Garlic Shrimp:
- In a large skillet, heat olive oil over medium-high heat. Add minced garlic and sauté for about 1 minute until fragrant.

Cook Shrimp:
- Add the shrimp to the skillet, spreading them in a single layer. Cook for 2-3 minutes on each side or until they turn pink and opaque.

Add Lemon and Seasonings:

- Add lemon zest, lemon juice, dried oregano, salt, pepper, and crushed red pepper flakes (if using). Stir to coat the shrimp with the lemony-garlic mixture. Cook for an additional 1-2 minutes.

Serve:
- Serve the Lemon Garlic Shrimp over a bed of cooked wild rice. Garnish with chopped fresh parsley.

This Lemon Garlic Shrimp with Wild Rice is a light and flavorful dish that brings together the citrusy brightness of lemon and the savory goodness of garlic. It's a quick and delicious meal that's perfect for a weeknight dinner. Enjoy!

Turkey and Cranberry Stuffed Bell Peppers with Wild Rice

Ingredients:

- 4 large bell peppers, halved and seeds removed
- 1 cup wild rice, cooked
- 1 pound ground turkey
- 1 onion, finely chopped
- 2 cloves garlic, minced
- 1/2 cup dried cranberries
- 1/2 cup chopped pecans or walnuts (optional)
- 1 teaspoon dried thyme
- Salt and pepper to taste
- 1 can (14 oz) diced tomatoes, drained
- 1 cup shredded mozzarella or cheddar cheese
- Fresh parsley, chopped, for garnish

Instructions:

Preheat Oven:
- Preheat the oven to 375°F (190°C).

Cook Wild Rice:
- Cook the wild rice according to package instructions. Set aside.

Prepare Bell Peppers:
- Cut the bell peppers in half lengthwise, removing seeds and membranes. Place the pepper halves in a baking dish.

Cook Turkey Mixture:
- In a large skillet, cook ground turkey over medium heat until browned. Add chopped onion and minced garlic, cooking until the onion is softened.

Add Cranberries and Nuts:
- Stir in dried cranberries, chopped nuts (if using), dried thyme, salt, and pepper. Cook for an additional 2-3 minutes.

Combine with Wild Rice:
- In a large bowl, combine the cooked wild rice with the turkey mixture. Add diced tomatoes and mix well.

Stuff Bell Peppers:
- Stuff each bell pepper half with the turkey and wild rice mixture, pressing down gently. Top each stuffed pepper with shredded cheese.

Bake:
- Cover the baking dish with foil and bake in the preheated oven for 25-30 minutes, or until the peppers are tender.

Broil (Optional):
- If desired, remove the foil and broil for an additional 2-3 minutes until the cheese is golden and bubbly.

Garnish and Serve:
- Garnish the Turkey and Cranberry Stuffed Bell Peppers with chopped fresh parsley before serving.

These Turkey and Cranberry Stuffed Bell Peppers with Wild Rice are a festive and flavorful dish, combining the savory flavors of turkey with the sweetness of cranberries. It's a perfect meal for holiday gatherings or any time you want a comforting and wholesome dish. Enjoy!

Millet Marvels:
Millet and Black Bean Salad

Ingredients:

For the Salad:

- 1 cup millet, rinsed
- 2 cups water
- 1 can (15 oz) black beans, drained and rinsed
- 1 cup corn kernels (fresh, frozen, or canned)
- 1 red bell pepper, diced
- 1/2 red onion, finely chopped
- 1 cup cherry tomatoes, halved
- 1/4 cup fresh cilantro, chopped
- 1 avocado, diced

For the Dressing:

- 3 tablespoons olive oil
- 2 tablespoons lime juice
- 1 teaspoon ground cumin
- 1 teaspoon chili powder
- Salt and pepper to taste

Instructions:

Cook Millet:
- In a saucepan, combine millet and water. Bring to a boil, then reduce heat to low, cover, and simmer for 15-20 minutes or until millet is tender and water is absorbed. Fluff with a fork and let it cool.

Prepare Vegetables:
- In a large bowl, combine cooked millet, black beans, corn, diced red bell pepper, chopped red onion, halved cherry tomatoes, chopped cilantro, and diced avocado.

Make Dressing:
- In a small bowl, whisk together olive oil, lime juice, ground cumin, chili powder, salt, and pepper to make the dressing.

Combine Ingredients:

- Pour the dressing over the salad ingredients and toss everything together until well coated.

Chill (Optional):
- Refrigerate the Millet and Black Bean Salad for at least 30 minutes to allow the flavors to meld. This step is optional but enhances the taste.

Serve:
- Serve the salad chilled or at room temperature. It can be enjoyed as a side dish or a light and satisfying main course.

This Millet and Black Bean Salad is a nutritious and vibrant dish with a mix of textures and flavors. It's perfect for a quick and healthy lunch or as a side dish for summer gatherings. Enjoy!

Millet-Stuffed Portobello Mushrooms

Ingredients:

For the Millet Stuffing:

- 1 cup millet, rinsed
- 2 cups vegetable broth or water
- 1 tablespoon olive oil
- 1 onion, finely chopped
- 2 cloves garlic, minced
- 1 carrot, finely diced
- 1 celery stalk, finely diced
- 1/2 cup frozen peas
- 1 teaspoon dried thyme
- Salt and pepper to taste
- 1/4 cup fresh parsley, chopped
- 1/4 cup grated Parmesan cheese (optional)

For the Portobello Mushrooms:

- 4 large portobello mushrooms, stems removed
- 2 tablespoons olive oil
- Salt and pepper to taste

Instructions:

Cook Millet:
- In a saucepan, combine millet and vegetable broth or water. Bring to a boil, then reduce heat to low, cover, and simmer for 15-20 minutes or until millet is tender and water is absorbed. Fluff with a fork and let it cool.

Prepare Portobello Mushrooms:
- Preheat the oven to 375°F (190°C). Place the portobello mushrooms on a baking sheet. Drizzle with olive oil and season with salt and pepper. Roast in the preheated oven for 15-20 minutes, or until the mushrooms are tender.

Sauté Vegetables:

- In a skillet, heat 1 tablespoon of olive oil over medium heat. Add chopped onion, minced garlic, diced carrot, and diced celery. Sauté until the vegetables are softened.

Combine Millet and Vegetables:
- Add the cooked millet, frozen peas, dried thyme, salt, and pepper to the skillet. Stir everything together and cook for an additional 2-3 minutes until the peas are heated through.

Add Fresh Parsley and Cheese:
- Remove the skillet from heat and stir in chopped fresh parsley. If desired, add grated Parmesan cheese and mix well.

Stuff Portobello Mushrooms:
- Spoon the millet mixture into the roasted portobello mushrooms, pressing down gently.

Bake:
- Return the stuffed portobello mushrooms to the oven and bake for an additional 10-15 minutes, or until everything is heated through.

Serve:
- Serve the Millet-Stuffed Portobello Mushrooms warm. Optionally, garnish with additional fresh parsley or Parmesan cheese.

These Millet-Stuffed Portobello Mushrooms are a flavorful and satisfying dish, perfect for a vegetarian main course or a delightful side. Enjoy the wholesome combination of millet and vegetables in each bite!

Lemon Millet Pilaf

Ingredients:

- 1 cup millet, rinsed
- 2 cups vegetable broth or water
- 2 tablespoons olive oil
- 1 onion, finely chopped
- 2 cloves garlic, minced
- Zest of 1 lemon
- Juice of 1 lemon
- 1/4 cup pine nuts, toasted
- 1/4 cup fresh parsley, chopped
- Salt and pepper to taste

Instructions:

Cook Millet:
- In a saucepan, combine millet and vegetable broth or water. Bring to a boil, then reduce heat to low, cover, and simmer for 15-20 minutes or until millet is tender and water is absorbed. Fluff with a fork and let it cool.

Sauté Onion and Garlic:
- In a large skillet, heat olive oil over medium heat. Add chopped onion and sauté until softened. Add minced garlic and continue to sauté for an additional 1-2 minutes.

Combine Millet and Aromatics:
- Stir in the cooked millet into the skillet with the sautéed onion and garlic.

Add Lemon Zest and Juice:
- Add lemon zest and lemon juice to the millet mixture. Stir well to combine.

Toast Pine Nuts:
- In a separate dry pan, toast the pine nuts over medium heat until they are golden brown. Keep a close eye on them to prevent burning.

Combine and Season:
- Add the toasted pine nuts and chopped fresh parsley to the millet mixture. Season with salt and pepper to taste. Toss everything together until well combined.

Serve:

- Serve the Lemon Millet Pilaf as a side dish or a light and refreshing main course. Optionally, garnish with additional lemon zest and parsley.

This Lemon Millet Pilaf is a bright and flavorful dish that pairs well with a variety of proteins or can be enjoyed on its own. The combination of citrusy lemon and nutty millet makes it a delightful addition to your meals. Enjoy!

Millet and Vegetable Stir-Fry

Ingredients:

- 1 cup millet, rinsed
- 2 cups vegetable broth or water
- 2 tablespoons soy sauce
- 1 tablespoon sesame oil
- 1 tablespoon olive oil
- 2 cloves garlic, minced
- 1 teaspoon ginger, grated
- 1 cup broccoli florets
- 1 bell pepper, thinly sliced
- 1 carrot, julienned
- 1 zucchini, sliced
- 1 cup snap peas, trimmed
- 2 green onions, sliced
- Sesame seeds for garnish (optional)

Instructions:

Cook Millet:
- In a saucepan, combine millet and vegetable broth or water. Bring to a boil, then reduce heat to low, cover, and simmer for 15-20 minutes or until millet is tender and water is absorbed. Fluff with a fork and set aside.

Prepare Sauce:
- In a small bowl, mix soy sauce and sesame oil. Set aside.

Stir-Fry Vegetables:
- Heat olive oil in a wok or large skillet over medium-high heat. Add minced garlic and grated ginger, sautéing for about 1 minute until fragrant.

Add Vegetables:
- Add broccoli florets, sliced bell pepper, julienned carrot, sliced zucchini, and snap peas to the wok. Stir-fry for 4-5 minutes until the vegetables are crisp-tender.

Combine with Millet:
- Add the cooked millet to the wok, pouring the soy sauce and sesame oil mixture over the vegetables and millet. Toss everything together until well combined.

Finish and Garnish:

- Stir in sliced green onions and cook for an additional 1-2 minutes. Optionally, garnish with sesame seeds.

Serve:
- Serve the Millet and Vegetable Stir-Fry hot. You can enjoy it as is or with additional protein like tofu, chicken, or shrimp if desired.

This Millet and Vegetable Stir-Fry is a wholesome and colorful dish that's quick to prepare. The nutty flavor of millet pairs well with the vibrant mix of stir-fried vegetables. Customize the recipe with your favorite veggies and enjoy a delicious and nutritious meal!

Millet Patties with Avocado Sauce

Ingredients:

For the Millet Patties:

- 1 cup millet, rinsed
- 2 cups vegetable broth or water
- 1/2 cup grated zucchini
- 1/4 cup grated carrot
- 1/4 cup finely chopped red onion
- 2 cloves garlic, minced
- 1 teaspoon ground cumin
- 1 teaspoon paprika
- Salt and pepper to taste
- 2 tablespoons olive oil (for cooking)

For the Avocado Sauce:

- 1 ripe avocado
- 1/4 cup Greek yogurt or sour cream
- 2 tablespoons fresh lemon juice
- 1 tablespoon fresh cilantro, chopped
- Salt and pepper to taste

Instructions:

Cook Millet:
- In a saucepan, combine millet and vegetable broth or water. Bring to a boil, then reduce heat to low, cover, and simmer for 15-20 minutes or until millet is tender and water is absorbed. Fluff with a fork and let it cool.

Prepare Avocado Sauce:
- In a blender or food processor, combine the flesh of the avocado, Greek yogurt or sour cream, fresh lemon juice, chopped cilantro, salt, and pepper. Blend until smooth. Adjust the seasoning to taste.

Make Millet Patties:
- In a large mixing bowl, combine the cooked millet, grated zucchini, grated carrot, chopped red onion, minced garlic, ground cumin, paprika, salt, and pepper. Mix well.

Form Patties:
- Form the mixture into patties, shaping them with your hands.

Cook Patties:
- Heat olive oil in a skillet over medium heat. Place the millet patties in the skillet and cook for about 4-5 minutes on each side or until golden brown.

Serve:
- Serve the Millet Patties hot, drizzled with the creamy Avocado Sauce.

These Millet Patties with Avocado Sauce make a flavorful and satisfying dish. The millet provides a nutty base, and the avocado sauce adds a creamy and zesty element. Enjoy these patties as a vegetarian main course or a delicious plant-based option!

Creamy Pumpkin Millet Porridge

Ingredients:

- 1 cup millet
- 3 cups water
- 1 cup canned pumpkin puree
- 2 cups milk (dairy or plant-based)
- 1/4 cup maple syrup or honey
- 1 teaspoon ground cinnamon
- 1/2 teaspoon ground nutmeg
- 1/4 teaspoon ground ginger
- 1/4 teaspoon salt
- 1 teaspoon vanilla extract
- Toppings: Chopped nuts, dried cranberries, or additional maple syrup (optional)

Instructions:

Cook Millet:
- In a saucepan, combine millet and water. Bring to a boil, then reduce heat to low, cover, and simmer for 15-20 minutes or until millet is tender and water is absorbed. Fluff with a fork and set aside.

Prepare Pumpkin Mixture:
- In a separate saucepan, combine pumpkin puree, milk, maple syrup or honey, ground cinnamon, ground nutmeg, ground ginger, and salt. Heat the mixture over medium heat, stirring occasionally.

Combine Millet and Pumpkin Mixture:
- Add the cooked millet to the pumpkin mixture and stir well. Continue cooking over medium heat until the porridge reaches your desired consistency.

Add Vanilla Extract:
- Stir in vanilla extract, adjusting sweetness to taste if necessary.

Serve:
- Ladle the Creamy Pumpkin Millet Porridge into bowls. Top with chopped nuts, dried cranberries, or a drizzle of additional maple syrup if desired.

Enjoy:
- Serve warm and enjoy the comforting flavors of this creamy pumpkin millet porridge.

This Creamy Pumpkin Millet Porridge is a wholesome and delicious breakfast option, especially during the fall and winter months. It's rich in flavor and provides a delightful combination of millet and pumpkin. Customize the toppings to your liking and savor this cozy dish!

Millet and Kale Soup

Ingredients:

- 1 cup millet, rinsed
- 2 tablespoons olive oil
- 1 onion, diced
- 2 carrots, diced
- 2 celery stalks, diced
- 3 cloves garlic, minced
- 1 teaspoon dried thyme
- 1 teaspoon dried rosemary
- 1 bay leaf
- 6 cups vegetable or chicken broth
- 1 can (15 oz) diced tomatoes, undrained
- 1 bunch kale, stems removed and leaves chopped
- Salt and pepper to taste
- Juice of 1 lemon
- Fresh parsley, chopped, for garnish (optional)
- Grated Parmesan cheese for serving (optional)

Instructions:

Sauté Vegetables:
- In a large pot, heat olive oil over medium heat. Add diced onion, carrots, and celery. Sauté until the vegetables are softened, about 5-7 minutes.

Add Garlic and Herbs:
- Add minced garlic, dried thyme, dried rosemary, and the bay leaf. Sauté for an additional 1-2 minutes until the garlic is fragrant.

Add Millet and Broth:
- Stir in the rinsed millet, vegetable or chicken broth, and diced tomatoes (with their juice). Bring the soup to a simmer.

Simmer Soup:
- Reduce heat to low, cover the pot, and let the soup simmer for about 20-25 minutes or until the millet is cooked and the vegetables are tender.

Add Kale:
- Add the chopped kale to the soup and simmer for an additional 5-7 minutes until the kale is wilted.

Season and Finish:
- Season the soup with salt and pepper to taste. Stir in the lemon juice for a bright finish.

Serve:
- Ladle the Millet and Kale Soup into bowls. Garnish with chopped fresh parsley and serve with grated Parmesan cheese if desired.

This Millet and Kale Soup is a wholesome and comforting dish that's perfect for colder days. The millet adds a nutty texture, and the kale provides a boost of nutrients. Enjoy this nutritious soup as a meal on its own or with a side of crusty bread.

Millet and Roasted Butternut Squash Bowl

Ingredients:

For the Roasted Butternut Squash:

- 1 small butternut squash, peeled, seeded, and diced
- 2 tablespoons olive oil
- 1 teaspoon ground cinnamon
- Salt and pepper to taste

For the Millet:

- 1 cup millet, rinsed
- 2 cups vegetable broth or water
- 1 tablespoon olive oil
- 1 teaspoon dried thyme
- Salt to taste

For the Bowl:

- 1 cup cooked chickpeas (canned or cooked from dried)
- 1/2 cup feta cheese, crumbled (optional)
- 1/4 cup pumpkin seeds (pepitas), toasted
- Fresh parsley, chopped, for garnish
- Balsamic glaze for drizzling (optional)

Instructions:

Roast Butternut Squash:
- Preheat the oven to 400°F (200°C). Toss diced butternut squash with olive oil, ground cinnamon, salt, and pepper. Spread on a baking sheet and roast in the preheated oven for 25-30 minutes or until the squash is tender and caramelized.

Cook Millet:
- In a saucepan, combine millet and vegetable broth or water. Bring to a boil, then reduce heat to low, cover, and simmer for 15-20 minutes or until millet is tender and water is absorbed. Fluff with a fork, stir in olive oil, dried thyme, and salt to taste.

Assemble the Bowl:

- In serving bowls, layer cooked millet, roasted butternut squash, cooked chickpeas, and crumbled feta cheese (if using).

Toast Pumpkin Seeds:
- In a dry pan, toast pumpkin seeds over medium heat until they are golden and fragrant.

Garnish and Drizzle:
- Sprinkle toasted pumpkin seeds and chopped fresh parsley over the bowl. Optionally, drizzle with balsamic glaze for extra flavor.

Serve:
- Serve the Millet and Roasted Butternut Squash Bowl warm. Enjoy the delicious combination of flavors and textures.

This Millet and Roasted Butternut Squash Bowl is a wholesome and satisfying meal that's perfect for a nutritious lunch or dinner. The roasted butternut squash adds sweetness, while the millet provides a nutty base. Customize the bowl with your favorite toppings and enjoy!

Millet Tabbouleh

Ingredients:

- 1 cup millet, rinsed
- 2 cups water
- 1 cup cherry tomatoes, diced
- 1 cucumber, diced
- 1/2 red onion, finely chopped
- 1 cup fresh parsley, chopped
- 1/4 cup fresh mint leaves, chopped
- Juice of 2 lemons
- 1/4 cup extra-virgin olive oil
- Salt and pepper to taste

Instructions:

Cook Millet:
- In a saucepan, combine millet and water. Bring to a boil, then reduce heat to low, cover, and simmer for 15-20 minutes or until millet is tender and water is absorbed. Fluff with a fork and let it cool.

Prepare Vegetables and Herbs:
- Dice the cherry tomatoes, cucumber, and finely chop the red onion. Chop fresh parsley and mint leaves.

Combine Ingredients:
- In a large mixing bowl, combine the cooked millet, diced tomatoes, diced cucumber, chopped red onion, chopped parsley, and chopped mint.

Make Dressing:
- In a small bowl, whisk together the lemon juice, extra-virgin olive oil, salt, and pepper to make the dressing.

Mix and Chill:
- Pour the dressing over the millet mixture and toss everything together until well coated. Refrigerate the Millet Tabbouleh for at least 30 minutes to allow the flavors to meld.

Serve:
- Serve the Millet Tabbouleh chilled. It makes a delicious and light side dish or a refreshing salad on its own.

This Millet Tabbouleh is a nutritious and flavorful twist on the classic tabbouleh, using millet as a base. The combination of fresh herbs, vegetables, and a zesty dressing creates a vibrant and satisfying dish. Enjoy the refreshing taste of this millet salad!

Millet and Chickpea Buddha Bowl

Ingredients:

For the Millet:

- 1 cup millet, rinsed
- 2 cups vegetable broth or water
- 1 tablespoon olive oil
- 1 teaspoon ground cumin
- Salt to taste

For the Chickpeas:

- 1 can (15 oz) chickpeas, drained and rinsed
- 1 tablespoon olive oil
- 1 teaspoon smoked paprika
- 1/2 teaspoon ground cumin
- Salt and pepper to taste

For the Buddha Bowl:

- Mixed greens or spinach
- Cherry tomatoes, halved
- Cucumber, sliced
- Avocado, sliced
- Carrot, shredded
- Red cabbage, shredded
- Hummus for serving
- Tahini dressing (optional)

Instructions:

Cook Millet:
- In a saucepan, combine millet and vegetable broth or water. Bring to a boil, then reduce heat to low, cover, and simmer for 15-20 minutes or until millet is tender and water is absorbed. Fluff with a fork, stir in olive oil, ground cumin, and salt to taste.

Roast Chickpeas:

- Preheat the oven to 400°F (200°C). In a bowl, toss chickpeas with olive oil, smoked paprika, ground cumin, salt, and pepper. Spread them on a baking sheet and roast for 20-25 minutes or until chickpeas are crispy.

Assemble Buddha Bowl:
- In serving bowls, arrange a portion of cooked millet, roasted chickpeas, mixed greens or spinach, cherry tomatoes, cucumber slices, avocado slices, shredded carrot, and shredded red cabbage.

Add Hummus:
- Spoon a dollop of hummus onto the bowl.

Drizzle with Dressing:
- Optionally, drizzle the Buddha Bowl with tahini dressing for extra flavor.

Serve:
- Serve the Millet and Chickpea Buddha Bowl immediately, allowing each person to customize their bowl according to preferences.

This Millet and Chickpea Buddha Bowl is a nutrient-packed and satisfying meal. It provides a variety of textures and flavors with the combination of millet, roasted chickpeas, fresh vegetables, and creamy hummus. Enjoy this wholesome and delicious Buddha Bowl!

Farro Feasts:
Farro and Vegetable Stir-Fry

Ingredients:

- 1 cup farro, rinsed and drained
- 2 cups vegetable broth or water
- 2 tablespoons soy sauce
- 1 tablespoon hoisin sauce
- 1 tablespoon sesame oil
- 1 tablespoon olive oil
- 3 cloves garlic, minced
- 1 tablespoon fresh ginger, grated
- 1 cup broccoli florets
- 1 bell pepper, thinly sliced
- 1 carrot, julienned
- 1 zucchini, sliced
- 1 cup snap peas, trimmed
- 2 green onions, sliced
- Sesame seeds for garnish
- Crushed red pepper flakes (optional, for heat)

Instructions:

Cook Farro:
- In a saucepan, combine farro and vegetable broth or water. Bring to a boil, then reduce heat to low, cover, and simmer for 25-30 minutes or until farro is tender. Drain any excess liquid.

Prepare Sauce:
- In a small bowl, whisk together soy sauce, hoisin sauce, and sesame oil. Set aside.

Stir-Fry Vegetables:
- Heat olive oil in a wok or large skillet over medium-high heat. Add minced garlic and grated ginger, sautéing for about 1 minute until fragrant.

Add Vegetables:
- Add broccoli florets, sliced bell pepper, julienned carrot, sliced zucchini, and snap peas to the wok. Stir-fry for 4-5 minutes until the vegetables are crisp-tender.

Add Cooked Farro:
- Add the cooked farro to the wok, pouring the soy sauce mixture over the vegetables and farro. Toss everything together until well combined.

Finish and Garnish:
- Stir in sliced green onions. Optionally, sprinkle sesame seeds and crushed red pepper flakes for extra flavor.

Serve:
- Serve the Farro and Vegetable Stir-Fry hot. Enjoy the delicious and nutritious combination of farro and colorful stir-fried vegetables.

This Farro and Vegetable Stir-Fry is a wholesome and satisfying dish that provides a perfect balance of grains and veggies. Customize the recipe with your favorite vegetables and enjoy a tasty and nutritious meal!

Farro and Italian Sausage Stuffed Peppers

Ingredients:

- 4 large bell peppers, halved and seeds removed
- 1 cup farro, rinsed and drained
- 2 cups vegetable broth or water
- 1 tablespoon olive oil
- 1 onion, finely chopped
- 2 cloves garlic, minced
- 1 pound Italian sausage, casings removed
- 1 can (14 oz) diced tomatoes, drained
- 1 teaspoon dried oregano
- 1 teaspoon dried basil
- Salt and pepper to taste
- 1 cup shredded mozzarella cheese
- Fresh parsley, chopped, for garnish

Instructions:

Preheat Oven:
- Preheat the oven to 375°F (190°C).

Cook Farro:
- In a saucepan, combine farro and vegetable broth or water. Bring to a boil, then reduce heat to low, cover, and simmer for 25-30 minutes or until farro is tender. Drain any excess liquid.

Sauté Onion and Garlic:
- In a large skillet, heat olive oil over medium heat. Add chopped onion and sauté until softened. Add minced garlic and cook for an additional 1-2 minutes.

Cook Italian Sausage:
- Add Italian sausage to the skillet, breaking it into crumbles with a spoon. Cook until browned and cooked through.

Combine Ingredients:
- Stir in cooked farro, drained diced tomatoes, dried oregano, dried basil, salt, and pepper. Mix well until all ingredients are combined.

Stuff Peppers:

- Arrange the halved bell peppers in a baking dish. Spoon the farro and Italian sausage mixture into each pepper half.

Bake:
- Sprinkle shredded mozzarella cheese over the stuffed peppers. Cover the baking dish with foil and bake in the preheated oven for 25-30 minutes, or until the peppers are tender.

Broil (Optional):
- If desired, remove the foil and broil for an additional 2-3 minutes until the cheese is golden and bubbly.

Garnish and Serve:
- Garnish the Farro and Italian Sausage Stuffed Peppers with chopped fresh parsley before serving.

These Farro and Italian Sausage Stuffed Peppers are a savory and satisfying dish, combining the nutty flavor of farro with the richness of Italian sausage. They make a delicious and comforting meal for any occasion. Enjoy!

Lemon Garlic Shrimp with Farro

Ingredients:

- 1 cup farro, rinsed and drained
- 2 cups vegetable broth or water
- 1 pound large shrimp, peeled and deveined
- 3 tablespoons olive oil
- 4 cloves garlic, minced
- Zest of 1 lemon
- Juice of 1 lemon
- 1 teaspoon dried oregano
- Salt and pepper to taste
- Fresh parsley, chopped, for garnish

Instructions:

Cook Farro:
- In a saucepan, combine farro and vegetable broth or water. Bring to a boil, then reduce heat to low, cover, and simmer for 25-30 minutes or until farro is tender. Drain any excess liquid.

Prepare Shrimp:
- In a bowl, toss the peeled and deveined shrimp with olive oil, minced garlic, lemon zest, lemon juice, dried oregano, salt, and pepper. Let it marinate for 10-15 minutes.

Cook Shrimp:
- Heat a large skillet over medium-high heat. Add the marinated shrimp to the skillet and cook for 2-3 minutes per side or until the shrimp are opaque and cooked through.

Combine Farro and Shrimp:
- Stir the cooked farro into the skillet with the cooked shrimp, allowing the flavors to combine. Cook for an additional 1-2 minutes.

Adjust Seasoning:
- Adjust the seasoning with salt, pepper, and additional lemon juice if needed.

Garnish and Serve:
- Garnish the Lemon Garlic Shrimp with chopped fresh parsley before serving.

This Lemon Garlic Shrimp with Farro is a quick and flavorful dish that combines the zesty taste of lemon with the savory goodness of garlic and perfectly cooked shrimp. It's a wholesome and satisfying meal that's easy to prepare. Enjoy!

Farro Salad with Roasted Vegetables and Feta

Ingredients:

For the Salad:

- 1 cup farro, rinsed and drained
- 2 cups water or vegetable broth
- 1 cup cherry tomatoes, halved
- 1 bell pepper, diced
- 1 zucchini, diced
- 1 red onion, thinly sliced
- 3 tablespoons olive oil
- Salt and pepper to taste
- 1/2 cup crumbled feta cheese
- Fresh basil or parsley, chopped, for garnish

For the Dressing:

- 3 tablespoons extra-virgin olive oil
- 2 tablespoons balsamic vinegar
- 1 teaspoon Dijon mustard
- 1 clove garlic, minced
- Salt and pepper to taste

Instructions:

Preheat Oven:
- Preheat the oven to 400°F (200°C).

Roast Vegetables:
- Place the cherry tomatoes, bell pepper, zucchini, and red onion on a baking sheet. Drizzle with olive oil, season with salt and pepper, and toss to coat. Roast in the preheated oven for 20-25 minutes or until the vegetables are tender and slightly caramelized.

Cook Farro:
- In a saucepan, combine farro and water or vegetable broth. Bring to a boil, then reduce heat to low, cover, and simmer for 25-30 minutes or until farro is tender. Drain any excess liquid.

Make Dressing:

- In a small bowl, whisk together extra-virgin olive oil, balsamic vinegar, Dijon mustard, minced garlic, salt, and pepper to make the dressing.

Assemble Salad:
- In a large bowl, combine the cooked farro, roasted vegetables, and crumbled feta cheese. Drizzle the dressing over the salad and toss gently to combine.

Garnish and Serve:
- Garnish the Farro Salad with chopped fresh basil or parsley. Serve it warm or at room temperature.

This Farro Salad with Roasted Vegetables and Feta is a delightful and nutritious dish that showcases the nutty flavor of farro alongside the sweetness of roasted vegetables and the creaminess of feta. It makes for a perfect side dish or a light and satisfying meal. Enjoy!

Creamy Mushroom and Spinach Farro Risotto

Ingredients:

- 1 cup farro, rinsed and drained
- 2 cups vegetable broth
- 2 tablespoons olive oil
- 1 onion, finely chopped
- 2 cloves garlic, minced
- 8 oz (about 225g) cremini or button mushrooms, sliced
- 1 cup baby spinach, chopped
- 1/2 cup dry white wine (optional)
- 1/2 cup grated Parmesan cheese
- 2 tablespoons unsalted butter
- Salt and pepper to taste
- Fresh parsley, chopped, for garnish

Instructions:

Prepare Farro:
- In a saucepan, bring the vegetable broth to a simmer. Add the farro and cook according to the package instructions until al dente. Drain any excess liquid.

Sauté Onion and Garlic:
- In a large skillet, heat olive oil over medium heat. Add chopped onion and sauté until softened. Add minced garlic and cook for an additional 1-2 minutes.

Cook Mushrooms:
- Add sliced mushrooms to the skillet and cook until they release their moisture and become golden brown.

Add Farro and Spinach:
- Stir in the cooked farro and chopped baby spinach. If using white wine, pour it into the skillet and cook until mostly evaporated.

Make it Creamy:
- Add grated Parmesan cheese and butter to the skillet. Stir continuously until the cheese and butter melt, creating a creamy texture. If needed, add a bit more vegetable broth for creaminess.

Season:

- Season the risotto with salt and pepper to taste. Adjust the consistency with more vegetable broth if desired.

Garnish and Serve:
- Garnish the Creamy Mushroom and Spinach Farro Risotto with chopped fresh parsley. Serve warm.

This Creamy Mushroom and Spinach Farro Risotto is a comforting and hearty dish that offers a unique twist on traditional risotto. The nutty flavor of farro pairs beautifully with the earthy mushrooms and vibrant spinach. Enjoy this wholesome and satisfying meal!

Farro and Pomegranate Salad

Ingredients:

For the Salad:

- 1 cup farro, rinsed and drained
- 2 cups water or vegetable broth
- 1 cup pomegranate arils (seeds)
- 1 cucumber, diced
- 1/2 cup crumbled feta cheese
- 1/4 cup chopped fresh mint leaves
- 1/4 cup chopped fresh parsley
- Salt and pepper to taste

For the Dressing:

- 3 tablespoons extra-virgin olive oil
- 2 tablespoons balsamic vinegar
- 1 teaspoon honey
- 1 teaspoon Dijon mustard
- Salt and pepper to taste

Instructions:

Cook Farro:
- In a saucepan, combine farro and water or vegetable broth. Bring to a boil, then reduce heat to low, cover, and simmer for 25-30 minutes or until farro is tender. Drain any excess liquid.

Prepare Dressing:
- In a small bowl, whisk together extra-virgin olive oil, balsamic vinegar, honey, Dijon mustard, salt, and pepper to make the dressing.

Assemble Salad:
- In a large bowl, combine the cooked farro, pomegranate arils, diced cucumber, crumbled feta cheese, chopped fresh mint, and chopped fresh parsley.

Add Dressing:

- Pour the dressing over the salad ingredients and toss gently to combine. Ensure the dressing evenly coats all the components.

Season:
- Season the Farro and Pomegranate Salad with salt and pepper to taste. Adjust the seasoning if needed.

Chill and Serve:
- Refrigerate the salad for at least 30 minutes to allow the flavors to meld. Serve chilled.

This Farro and Pomegranate Salad is a delightful and nutritious dish that combines the hearty texture of farro with the burst of sweetness from pomegranate arils. The fresh herbs and feta cheese add a burst of flavor. Enjoy this vibrant salad as a side or a light meal!

Farro and Lentil Soup

Ingredients:

- 1 cup farro, rinsed
- 1 cup dried green or brown lentils, rinsed and drained
- 1 onion, diced
- 2 carrots, diced
- 2 celery stalks, diced
- 3 cloves garlic, minced
- 1 can (14 oz) diced tomatoes
- 8 cups vegetable broth
- 1 teaspoon ground cumin
- 1 teaspoon smoked paprika
- 1 bay leaf
- Salt and pepper to taste
- 2 cups fresh spinach or kale, chopped
- Juice of 1 lemon
- Olive oil for drizzling (optional)
- Fresh parsley, chopped, for garnish

Instructions:

Sauté Vegetables:
- In a large soup pot, heat olive oil over medium heat. Add diced onion, carrots, and celery. Sauté until the vegetables are softened, about 5-7 minutes.

Add Lentils and Farro:
- Stir in rinsed lentils and farro. Cook for an additional 2-3 minutes.

Add Garlic and Spices:
- Add minced garlic, ground cumin, smoked paprika, and bay leaf. Sauté for 1-2 minutes until the garlic is fragrant.

Pour in Broth:
- Pour in the vegetable broth and add the diced tomatoes (with their juice). Bring the soup to a simmer.

Simmer Soup:
- Reduce heat to low, cover the pot, and let the soup simmer for about 25-30 minutes or until the lentils and farro are tender.

Season:
- Season the soup with salt and pepper to taste. Adjust the seasoning as needed.

Add Greens and Lemon Juice:
- Stir in chopped fresh spinach or kale and the juice of one lemon. Cook for an additional 2-3 minutes until the greens are wilted.

Serve:
- Ladle the Farro and Lentil Soup into bowls. Drizzle with olive oil if desired and garnish with chopped fresh parsley.

This Farro and Lentil Soup is a wholesome and filling dish that's rich in fiber and nutrients. The combination of farro, lentils, and vegetables creates a comforting and nutritious soup. Enjoy it on a chilly day for a satisfying and flavorful meal!

Mediterranean Farro Bowl

Ingredients:

For the Farro:

- 1 cup farro, rinsed and drained
- 2 cups vegetable broth or water
- 1 tablespoon olive oil
- Salt to taste

For the Bowl:

- 1 cup cherry tomatoes, halved
- 1 cucumber, diced
- 1/2 red onion, thinly sliced
- 1/2 cup Kalamata olives, pitted and sliced
- 1/2 cup feta cheese, crumbled
- 1/4 cup fresh parsley, chopped

For the Dressing:

- 3 tablespoons extra-virgin olive oil
- 1 tablespoon red wine vinegar
- 1 teaspoon dried oregano
- Salt and pepper to taste

Instructions:

Cook Farro:
- In a saucepan, combine farro and vegetable broth or water. Bring to a boil, then reduce heat to low, cover, and simmer for 25-30 minutes or until farro is tender. Drain any excess liquid and toss with olive oil. Season with salt to taste.

Prepare Vegetables:

- In a large bowl, combine cherry tomatoes, diced cucumber, thinly sliced red onion, Kalamata olives, crumbled feta cheese, and chopped fresh parsley.

Make Dressing:
- In a small bowl, whisk together extra-virgin olive oil, red wine vinegar, dried oregano, salt, and pepper to make the dressing.

Assemble the Bowl:
- Divide the cooked farro among serving bowls. Top with the prepared vegetable mixture.

Drizzle with Dressing:
- Drizzle the Mediterranean Farro Bowl with the prepared dressing.

Toss and Serve:
- Toss the ingredients gently in each bowl to combine. Serve immediately.

This Mediterranean Farro Bowl is a colorful and flavorful dish that highlights the vibrant ingredients of Mediterranean cuisine. The combination of farro, fresh vegetables, olives, and feta creates a wholesome and satisfying meal. Enjoy this bowl for a nutritious and delicious lunch or dinner!

Chicken and Farro Skillet

Ingredients:

- 1 cup farro, rinsed and drained
- 2 cups chicken broth
- 1 tablespoon olive oil
- 1 pound boneless, skinless chicken breasts, cut into bite-sized pieces
- Salt and pepper to taste
- 1 onion, finely chopped
- 2 cloves garlic, minced
- 1 bell pepper, diced
- 1 zucchini, diced
- 1 teaspoon dried thyme
- 1 teaspoon paprika
- 1/2 teaspoon cayenne pepper (optional for heat)
- 1 can (14 oz) diced tomatoes, undrained
- 1 cup frozen peas
- Fresh parsley, chopped, for garnish

Instructions:

Cook Farro:
- In a saucepan, combine farro and chicken broth. Bring to a boil, then reduce heat to low, cover, and simmer for 20-25 minutes or until farro is tender and liquid is absorbed.

Sauté Chicken:
- In a large skillet, heat olive oil over medium-high heat. Season chicken pieces with salt and pepper, then add them to the skillet. Cook until browned on all sides and cooked through. Remove chicken from the skillet and set aside.

Sauté Vegetables:
- In the same skillet, add chopped onion, minced garlic, diced bell pepper, and diced zucchini. Sauté until vegetables are softened.

Season and Add Tomatoes:
- Stir in dried thyme, paprika, and cayenne pepper (if using). Add the diced tomatoes with their juice, breaking them up with a spoon.

Combine Chicken and Farro:

- Return the cooked chicken to the skillet and add the cooked farro. Mix everything together to combine.

Add Peas:
- Stir in frozen peas and cook for an additional 3-5 minutes until peas are heated through.

Adjust Seasoning:
- Adjust the seasoning with salt and pepper to taste.

Garnish and Serve:
- Garnish the Chicken and Farro Skillet with chopped fresh parsley and serve hot.

This Chicken and Farro Skillet is a well-balanced and flavorful one-pan meal that combines protein, whole grains, and vegetables. It's quick to prepare and perfect for a wholesome weeknight dinner. Enjoy!

Farro and Asparagus Risotto

Ingredients:

- 1 cup farro, rinsed and drained
- 2 cups vegetable broth
- 1 bunch asparagus, tough ends trimmed and cut into bite-sized pieces
- 2 tablespoons olive oil
- 1 onion, finely chopped
- 2 cloves garlic, minced
- 1 cup dry white wine
- 1/2 cup grated Parmesan cheese
- Salt and pepper to taste
- Fresh lemon zest for garnish
- Fresh parsley, chopped, for garnish

Instructions:

Prepare Farro:
- In a saucepan, bring the vegetable broth to a simmer. Add the farro and cook according to the package instructions until al dente. Drain any excess liquid.

Blanch Asparagus:
- In a separate pot of boiling water, blanch the asparagus pieces for 2-3 minutes until they are bright green and slightly tender. Drain and immediately plunge them into ice water to stop the cooking process. Set aside.

Sauté Onion and Garlic:
- In a large skillet, heat olive oil over medium heat. Add chopped onion and sauté until softened. Add minced garlic and cook for an additional 1-2 minutes.

Cook Farro in Wine:
- Stir in the drained farro and cook for 1-2 minutes. Pour in the dry white wine and cook until the wine is mostly absorbed.

Add Asparagus:
- Add the blanched asparagus to the skillet and stir to combine with the farro.

Gradually Add Broth:

- Begin adding the simmering vegetable broth, one ladle at a time, stirring frequently. Allow the liquid to be absorbed before adding the next ladle. Continue this process until the farro is creamy and cooked to your desired tenderness.

Finish and Add Cheese:
- Stir in the grated Parmesan cheese, and season the risotto with salt and pepper to taste.

Garnish and Serve:
- Garnish the Farro and Asparagus Risotto with fresh lemon zest and chopped parsley. Serve warm.

This Farro and Asparagus Risotto is a delightful twist on the classic, using nutty farro and fresh asparagus to create a wholesome and flavorful dish. Enjoy this creamy and comforting risotto as a main course or a side dish!

www.ingramcontent.com/pod-product-compliance
Lightning Source LLC
LaVergne TN
LVHW081551060526
838201LV00054B/1857